DEVELOPING
INVITING
SCHOOLS

DEVELOPING INVITING SCHOOLS

A Beneficial Framework for Teaching and Leading

William W. Purkey
John M. Novak
Joan R. Fretz

TEACHERS COLLEGE PRESS

TEACHERS COLLEGE | COLUMBIA UNIVERSITY

NEW YORK AND LONDON

Published by Teachers College Press,® 1234 Amsterdam Avenue, New York, NY 10027

Copyright © 2020 by Teachers College, Columbia University

Front cover photo by Yuttana Contributor Studio, Shutterstock.

Library of Congress Cataloging-in-Publication Data is available at loc.gov

ISBN 978-0-8077-6472-5 (paper)
ISBN 978-0-8077-6473-2 (hardcover)
ISBN 978-0-8077-7925-5 (ebook)

Printed on acid-free paper
Manufactured in the United States of America

*Dedicated to Peter Wong, CK Fung, Clio Chan,
and all our Hong Kong colleagues who have adopted
Invitational Education as their guiding theory of practice.*

*We give a special salute to Betty L. Siegel,
co-founder of The International Alliance for Invitational Education,
for her dynamic and inspiring leadership.*

*Finally, we dedicate this book to all educators,
past, present, and future, who have been, now are,
and will be developing inviting schools.*

Contents

Preface

Dear Colleague,

The following *Professional Standards for Educational Leaders* (2015) set high expectations for educational leaders. Fortunately, when using the invitational framework presented in this book, teachers and leaders will find success in each of the ten standards. When developing an inviting school, all staff members have the opportunity to lead—in the classroom, cafeteria, and hallways, as well as conference rooms and offices. So, you will contribute to the process as leaders.

Here are a few examples of how invitational teaching and leading will enable you and your colleagues to meet these Professional Standards by developing a beneficial social and emotional climate in your schools.

1. ***Mission, vision, and core values.*** *Developing Inviting Schools* presents the core values of invitational leadership: respect, trust, care, optimism, and intentionality. Our mission is to create, sustain, and enhance truly caring and welcoming schools. Our vision is that human potential, not always apparent, is always there, waiting to be discovered and invited forth. Fundamentally, education is an imaginative act of hope.
2. ***Ethics and Professional Norms.*** The democratic ethos is the primary foundation of an invitational approach to educational leadership. A detailed description of ethical leadership is presented in Chapter 2.
3. ***Equity and Cultural Responsiveness.*** The theme of *Developing Inviting Schools* is that everyone matters. People are seen as able, valuable, and responsible, and treated accordingly. Improving the human condition for everyone is a moral imperative.
4. ***Curriculum, Instruction, and Assessment.*** *Developing Inviting Schools* focuses on how instruction is presented, discussed, perceived, and assessed. We maintain that the process is the product in the making.
5. ***Community of Care and Support for Students.*** To invite is to summon cordially, not to shun, to offer something beneficial for consideration, instead of relying on rewards and consequences. This is what inviting schools are all about.

6. ***Professional Capacity of School Personnel.*** The beliefs of professionals in the school will influence the ways they see themselves, their students, and the world. We believe all school adults can benefit from using an invitational approach to communicating.

7. ***Professional Community for Teachers and Staff.*** This book stresses the interdependence of everyone in the school. Its focus on the democratic ethos and being professionally inviting with others is all about professional community.

8. ***Meaningful Engagement of Families and Community.*** Making schools a place where people want to teach and learn is a central message of this book. This involves inviting all stakeholders to make schools inviting places to be.

9. ***Operations and Management.*** *Developing Inviting Schools* provides a defensible theory of practice for school leaders as they make decisions regarding how their organization will operate and be managed. This theory of practice goes deeper than surface-level initiatives, so that what is done is ethically and educationally defensible.

10. ***School Improvement.*** Efforts to improve the school are done systemically by considering the "Five Powerful Ps": People, Places, Policies, Programs, and Processes. A systematic roadmap for school improvement, called the HELIX, is provided in Chapter 7.

By using the invitational framework, you'll be grounding each standard in a defensible and sustainable theory of practice that will enable you to move forward with and beyond each goal. During times of crisis, developing inviting schools is paramount.

William W. Purkey
John M. Novak
Joan R. Fretz

DEVELOPING INVITING SCHOOLS

CHAPTER 1

Introducing Invitational Education

The beauty of the Invitational Education framework is that it is simple enough to keep in your head, yet profound changes can occur if it is applied personally and professionally with intentionality, keeping the elements of care, trust, respect, and optimism in mind.

—Melissa Cain, professor, University of Findlay,
personal communication, August 15, 2016

Does your school have a positive climate? Ask any school leader and they will tell you about the endless list of projects, programs, and assemblies being done with students and staff every year. Yet, if you ask staff members, students, parents, and visitors if the school treats them as able, valuable, and responsible members of the school community, they often share reasons why their answer is "Not really." Does your school invite success? Most schools fall far short of this ideal.

Developing Inviting Schools describes how everybody and everything within and outside the school constitute a signal system. These signals communicate messages that inform people that they are able, valuable, and responsible, or unable, valueless, and irresponsible. Without a clear understanding of how this massive communication system works, we run the risk of swinging back and forth on the pendulum of school improvement. This book is our effort to put into action a theory of practice for implementing an intentionally beneficial approach to teaching and leading—one that feels right, makes sense, and leads to sustained improvement. We call this attempt *Invitational Education*, and describe what it is, why it is needed, and how it has been put into practice in schools around the world.

This book is based on the position that the primary mission of schools is to summon individuals cordially and ethically to realize their relatively untapped potential in all worthwhile areas of human endeavor. Accomplishing this mission requires educators who are *intentionally* caring, respectful, trusting, and optimistic with themselves and others, personally and professionally. Their task is to create a school where policies are fair-minded, processes are democratic, programs are inclusive, places are safe and attractive, and most importantly, people are caring professionals.

The journey to developing a truly inviting school involves going beyond present patterns of thinking about creating and sustaining safe schools. It goes beyond the organizational and managerial processes and programs that are based primarily on patterns of security and authority. Now more than ever, it is vital that we go beyond physical safety to give attention to the social and emotional world of our students and staff. A specific concern of educators is how to address the myriad array of real-life factors in the school ecosystem. This book provides a tested and reliable framework for creating, sustaining, and enhancing schools that are socially and emotionally good places for people to be.

The need for this book is self-evident. Educators at every level and location are searching for ways to deal with the vast array of real-life challenges. They wonder where to begin, how to get buy-in from staff and students, and how to address root causes of each problem. This book provides the promise of Invitational Education as a way to think and act more deeply about what schools can and should be about. The value of this book is that it offers a defensible theory of practice that is enduring. Too often, movements in education are short-lived. Like a circus, they roll into town, set up their tents, promise good things, then pack up and leave without a trace. These approaches to school improvement, while well-meaning, lack a consistent and enduring vision of what the school wants to accomplish. *Developing Inviting Schools* provides a clear path to school transformation that can be understood and shared by every adult in the school. This approach is called Invitational Education. It is a simple—but not simplistic—framework for addressing our greatest challenges in making sustainable and worthwhile changes in schools. Because it benefits everyone in the school, it is likely to be accepted and adopted by everyone. The present concern with school safety provides an illustration of how Invitational Education works in the real world of schools.

In response to horrific gun violence in schools, most law enforcement and educational leaders have relied on traditional law enforcement processes These include shakedowns of student lockers and backpacks, along with armed officers patrolling the hallways. This is accompanied by frequent "lockdown" drills where teachers lock and barricade their classroom doors, turn off the lights, and have the students hide in a corner. Unfortunately, these law-enforcement measures, along with millions of school budget dollars being spent on building security systems, are now the new norm. Jonathan Hillard, 4th-grade teacher at Apollo Elementary School in Titusville, Florida, expressed his dismay about this new climate of high alert poignantly: "I want to be able to see parents walking in and out of schools and not feel like they're suspects. I want our schools to be schools. I don't want them to be hardened military facilities" (Samples, 2018).

The new norm is accompanied by the old norms of lack of student involvement in school activities; lack of student relationships with fellow students; and lack of meaningful teacher, counselor, parent, and other adult caregiver support. This lack is compounded by the unrelenting pressures of high-stakes testing, the need to "be the best," the turnover of school personnel, the suspension or expulsion of students for even minor infractions, along with the ever-present pressure of social media and bullying by mean-spirited students.

Many of the violent rampages in schools originated within the school environment. If the main focus is on locking the doors and controlling students, schools are simply locking the problem inside. If the primary approach to discipline is exclusionary, then schools are increasing the isolation and disengagement from school that may cause a student to choose violence. Most experts on school violence agree that fostering positive social, emotional, and academic success for all students is vital. In response to recent school shootings, leading authorities (Astor et al., 2018) have called for "all schools to maintain physically and emotionally safe conditions and positive school environments," and have expressed the need to "reform school discipline to reduce exclusionary practices and foster positive social, behavioral, emotional, and academic success for students." While this "call to action" is not new, specialists still fail to explain how to create and sustain a positive school climate.

The challenge encountered by many school leaders is that they lack a defensible theory of practice to guide their efforts. They struggle with *how* to create and sustain a school climate and culture that supports all involved and helps them to thrive. Making this happen involves the intentional action of everyone in the school community. Invitational Education provides a framework to help us become more perceptive and skillful in our choice of words and actions, and more aware of how we, and everything in our school, influences what others believe to be true about themselves, and in turn, their choices of behavior.

> *The challenge encountered by many school leaders is that they lack a defensible theory of practice to guide their efforts.*

Most everyone would agree that motivation is a key factor in successful education. What is elusive is a way to think about motivation that respects the individuality of each person and their unique way of making sense of the world. With this in mind, it will be helpful at the beginning of this first chapter to consider the nature of motivation as presented in this book. We build from the position that every living person is continuously motivated. There is no such thing as an unmotivated person. People may not do what we want them to do, but that does not mean they are unmotivated. It simply means that they don't want to do what we want. There may be physical, social, or emotional factors that in their mind take priority. Motivation is a continuous drive that exists within every living person, at all times and places. This basic human drive is to maintain, protect, and enhance the perceived self—the picture a person has of who they are and how they fit in the world. This definition of motivation is a tremendously freeing concept. It allows educators to think with a *"doing with"* as opposed to a *"doing to"* mindset. It means that educators can spend their time influencing what direction this intrinsic motivation might take. As an analogy, the student's engine is running. The role of educators, and education itself, is to build good roads, remove the roadblocks, set out directional signs, and help the students learn to drive safely. Students are more likely to drive safely and sanely when they believe that good driving will benefit themselves. With a "doing with" mindset, educators can invite students and staff members to realize their relatively limitless possibilities in all areas of human endeavor.

As this book is written, school climate is being greatly influenced by the terrible COVID-19 pandemic. Students and faculty are faced with the constant demands of keeping 6 feet apart and wearing masks that hide our facial expressions. Learning is interrupted with frequent reminders of social distancing and proper hygiene, while everyone remains fearful of interactions that might threaten their health as well as that of their families. Without intentional and constant care, schools run the risk of being grim and joyless places. This culture of uncertainty cries out for socially and emotionally focused schools.

THE INFLUENCE OF INVITATIONAL EDUCATION

Try as we might, what should be obvious is that this book cannot solve every problem that educators face in the real world. Situations can be too complex, and where to begin can be difficult to pinpoint. However, problems are more likely to become opportunities for growth when viewed from the lens of Invitational Education. There is no absolute guarantee that an inviting school will reduce potential dangers. However, there is a much greater possibility that a "disinviting" school is far more likely to experience isolation and disengagement.

The positive influence of Invitational Education can first be measured by the HELIX, presented in Chapter 7. As explained in the HELIX, change typically goes through four steps: (1) awareness, (2) understanding, (3) application, and (4) adoption. The first sign of significant change in a school is when people who live and work there become *aware* of a better way to have a school. By asking anyone in the school if they are aware of Invitational Education, a positive answer is a measure that something good is beginning to happen in the school. To determine the effectiveness of education by immediately looking for adoption is vastly premature. Expecting a school to adopt Invitational Education as its guiding principle is like expecting a small sapling, planted in the morning, to provide shade at noon. Invitational Education is a slow but sure 12-step reflective process.

The second way to measure the influence of Invitational Education is to use the Inviting School Survey-Revised (2016), developed by Ken Smith at Australian Catholic University (Appendix B). The survey is a behaviorally anchored 50-item questionnaire designed to identify aspects of the school that are inviting or "disinviting." The purpose of the ISS-R is to provide educators with an instrument that identifies how the five dimensions of a school (People, Places, Program, Policies, and Processes) are influencing the total climate of the school. The ISS-R is designed for use by all stakeholders in the school, including students ages 8 or older, parents, teachers, administrators, counselors, and the support staff.

A psychometric analysis of an adaptation of the Inviting School Survey was conducted by Shoffner and Vacc (1999). The Inviting School Safety Survey is a modification of the Inviting School Survey that includes items on school safety. The researchers concluded that the factor structure (People, Places, Policies, Programs, and Processes—the 5 Ps) of the survey addresses the underlying theory of Invitational Education and can be used to assess the perceived environment of a school. The survey can provide a potential framework for measuring interventions that are intended to improve feelings of safety and freedom from violent acts.

Although this entire book is dedicated to defining and explaining Invitational Education, in a nutshell it is a way of seeing and understanding what really takes place in schools. Its goal is to penetrate to the deeper culture that is at the very heart of the school. Invitational Education is an ethical art and craft, intentionally built on care, optimism, respect, and trust. It is designed to summon every person who enters a school building to see themselves as able, valuable, and responsible, and to act accordingly. At heart, Invitational Education is a way of thinking about and acting on matters of importance. By doing so it connects theoretical formulations with practical, real-life concerns and helps develop a shared mindset and way of communicating that pervades every aspect of the school.

> *Do the people, places, policies, programs, and processes add to, or subtract from, the primary goal of making this school a better place for people?*

Invitational Education maintains that the quality of life in schools is vital in itself and goes beyond school safety and academic achievement. Fortunately, a socially and emotionally safe climate adds significantly to both school safety and academic success. It also makes schools places where people want to be and learn—schools that are an essential part of a caring society.

In the inviting school, there is one litmus test that governs everything that happens. Everything in the school is measured by a simple question: Do the people, places, policies, programs, and processes add to, or subtract from, the primary goal of making this school a better place for people? In the inviting school, everything counts.

Just as everyone and everything in hospitals should encourage healing, everyone and everything in schools should invite the realizing of positive educational goals. The Five Powerful Ps of Invitational Education involve the *people* (teachers, administrators, supervisors, counselors, assistants, bus drivers, cafeteria staff, secretaries, librarians, nurses, security officers, custodians, crossing guards), the *places* (classrooms, offices, hallways, commons, restrooms, computer labs, playing fields, gymnasiums, libraries), the *policies* (rules, codes, procedures), the *programs* (curricular or co-curricular), and the *processes* (the spirit or flavor of the way things are done). The formulation, realization, and evaluation of this concept has been named Invitational Education.

Invitational Education values practice-based evidence as well as evidence-based practice. Recently, the importance of producing practice-based evidence to guide and inform the development of interventions has been widely recognized (Adelman & Taylor, 2014; Ammerman et al., 2014; Green, 2008). If innovations do not play effective roles in the real-life ecosystem of a classroom or school, educators will not view the innovation as valuable or useful. Chapter 8 provides strong practice-based research on the efficacy of Invitational Education. Dr. Jenny Edwards at Fielding University in Colorado has compiled over 300 studies that are primarily practice-based investigations that deal with a broad array of real-life issues. Sixty-five of these studies are doctoral dissertations. In addition, the International Alliance for Invitational Education (IAIE), a worldwide, nonprofit organization, has recognized to date over 400 schools with the IAIE Inviting School Award, and 94 Inviting School Fidelity Awards for schools that have maintained their commitment to Invitational Education for 2 to 17 years. Many other schools that have not continued participation in the award program have also actively sustained their use of Invitational Education. The practice-based evidence supporting Invitational Education is ample.

Invitational Education focuses on five domains that exist in practically every environment and that contribute to the success or failure of each individual. The 5 Ps make up the ecosystem in which individuals continuously interact. A starfish analogy (see Figure 1.1) is used to illustrate how the 5 Ps, applied with steady and persistent pressure, will overcome the biggest challenges in an organization. Just as the starfish gently and continuously uses each of its arms in turn, to keep sustained pressure on the one oyster muscle until it eventually opens, so will organizations meet their challenges successfully by paying close attention to the 5 Ps.

In considering the 5 Ps it is obvious that Invitational Education is far more than "being nice," "giving praise," providing awards for good behavior, or distributing signs to students that read "I am lovable and

Figure 1.1. Starfish Analogy

POLICIES
Inclusive
Fair
Equitable
Tolerant
Defensible
Consistent
Flexible
Just

PROCESSES
Academic
Democratic
Interdisciplinary
Encouraging
Positive
Cooperative
Collaborative
Engaging

PEOPLE
Trusting
Respectful
Optimistic
Caring
Non-judgmental
Accessible
Courteous
International

PLACES
Functional
Attractive
Clean
Efficient
Aesthetic
Safe
Welcoming
Personal

PROGRAMS
Enriching
Stimulating
Healthful
Interactive
Constructive
Personalized
Inclusive
Ingenious

INVITATIONAL EDUCATION

capable." While positive social interactions are important, they are only a small part of Invitational Education. Figure 1.1 provides some inviting characteristics for the five domains.

The opening chapters of *Developing Inviting Schools* introduce Invitational Education and describe its ethical and psychological foundations. Later chapters present practical, how-to material that demonstrates ways of translating theory into practice. Throughout this book we use the term "teacher" and "leader" to include everyone in the school who comes in contact with the students. Each and every school employee has the potential to be a profound beneficial presence in the lives of students. From the perspective of Invitational Education, everyone in the school is a teacher.

AN EVOLVING THEORY OF PRACTICE

Invitational Education is an ethical theory of professional and personal practice that influences the well-being of all who are involved in educating—students, teachers, administrators, support staff, and parents—and that intentionally seeks to create, sustain, and enhance total learning environments based on trust, respect, optimism, and care. A theory of practice is a way of thinking about that which is considered worth doing well. Invitational Education is thus a general and focused framework for thinking and acting about what is believed to be worthwhile in schools. As a developing theory of practice, Invitational Education is incomplete, with questions unanswered and avenues unexplored. Invitational Education is an evolving concept. It points to a promising direction, offers an ethically principled approach to the educative process, encourages a common language of improvement, and provides systematic and practical ways to make schools "the most inviting places in town."

Getting to the basics, Invitational Education is a democratically oriented, perceptually anchored self-concept approach to the educative process that centers on five basic assumptions, which are laid out in Figure 1.2.

The five assumptions of Invitational Education both focus and constrain educators to operate democratically:

- *First*, believing in the ability, value, and responsibility of each person commits educators to developing ethical approaches that summon students to take ownership of their learning.
- *Second*, the collaborative, cooperative nature of the teaching/learning process is emphasized in the "doing-with" nature of inviting. This means that in some meaningful way, teachers and students are "in this together."
- *Third*, saying "the process is the product in the making" means that how one goes about doing something affects what the result will be, because the process lives on, at least in the memories of those who deliver the product.
- *Fourth*, the belief in human potential assumes that everyone is using only a part of their many potentials and possibilities.
- *Fifth*, the idea that every person and everything in and around schools adds to, or subtracts from, the process of being a beneficial presence in the lives of human beings means that people and environments are never neutral; they are either summoning or shunning the development of human potential.

Ideally, the factors of people, places, policies, programs, and processes should be so intentionally inviting as to create a world in which each person is cordially summoned to develop intellectually, socially, physically,

Figure 1.2. Invitational Education Assumptions

The five assumptions of Invitational Education both focus and constrain educators to operate democratically:

1. People are able, valuable, and responsible and should be treated accordingly.
2. Educating should be a collaborative, cooperative activity.
3. The process is the product in the making.
4. People possess untapped potential in all areas of worthwhile human endeavor.
5. This potential can best be realized by places, policies, programs, and processes specifically designed to invite development and by people who are intentionally inviting with themselves and others, personally and professionally.

psychologically, and morally. This is a lot to expect from all involved in the educative process. However, to expect less is to diminish hope in people, their potential, and the educative process. Without the possibility of imaginative acts of hope, the vibrant creative energy of schools is lost, and people are, at best, merely going through the motions.

With these five assumptions as a theoretical focal point, the practice of Invitational Education is based on developing, transmitting, and evaluating caring, proactive, and responsible messages. Messages are the basic unit in Invitational Education. Based on an understanding of messages as considered/not considered; intended/not intended; extended/not extended; received/not received; evaluated/not evaluated, educational situations are studied, and ethically principled strategies are suggested, put into practice, modified, and evaluated. As detailed by Novak et al. (2014), with this communicative framework, Invitational Education proponents can move from the personal to the societal by attending to how people talk to themselves and others, think about and develop curricula, work in schools, and act in and through public institutions.

A SYSTEMATIC APPROACH

Invitational Education provides educators with a systematic and sequential understanding of the social and emotional climate of schools. This understanding of the depth and breadth of messages is used to develop environments and ways of life that are anchored in attitudes of respect, care, and civility and that encourage the realization of democratic goals. It is important to note that although Invitational Education can be applied in many ways, it is not simply doing whatever feels good. Invitational Education is a self-correcting system that seeks to integrate—in creative and ethical ways—research, theory, and practice. It is an attempt to integrate educators' deepest feelings, their clearest thoughts, and their sustained actions.

The term Invitational Education was chosen because the two words have special meaning. Our English word *invite* is probably a derivative of the Latin word *invitare*, which can mean "to offer something beneficial for consideration." Translated literally, invitare means "to summon cordially, not to shun." The word *education* comes from the Latin word *educare*, which means to "draw out" or "call forth" something potential or latent. Literally, then, Invitational Education is the process by which people are cordially summoned to realize their potential in all areas of worthwhile human endeavor. Implied in Invitational Education is a commitment to respectful treatment and positive growth.

The concept of potential is essential for a thorough understanding of education. Potential, as used in Invitational Education, is not some pre-formed destiny existing within the individual. The script has not already been written. *Invitational Education is the process by which people are cordially summoned to realize their potential in all areas of worthwhile human endeavor.* Rather, potential refers to the energies and interests of people that can be connected to worthwhile opportunities that encourage exploration, refinement, and further possibilities for growth. With this view of potential in mind, Invitational Education practitioners work toward developing caring behaviors, nurturing environments, person-centered policies, engaging programs, and democratic processes. These people aim to create an educational culture that summons everyone involved to lead educational lives.

What, then, is Invitational Education? Although this entire book is an answer to this question, this opening chapter provides an explanation of some of Invitational Education's basic concepts and principles. Various aspects of Invitational Education, along with practical applications, are presented throughout this book. The key to school improvement is people, with ideas they want to put into practice. It is imperative that people in schools re-examine the ways in which they conduct their day-to-day activities and interactions.

THE PROMISE OF INVITATIONAL EDUCATION

To promise is to form a covenant. The authors of this book seek to form a covenant with the reader. We believe that Invitational Education will provide the reader with a practice-based guide to creating, sustaining, and enhancing truly caring and welcoming schools.

This book addresses the concerns and hopes of an array of real people in real situations. As mentioned earlier, practice-based evidence is as important as evidence-based practice. The failure of many national efforts to improve schools, such as *No Child Left Behind, Race to the Top,* and the *What Works Clearinghouse* is that they overlooked the people in the process. Traditional efforts to improve schools tend to focus on current practices and standard procedures. The qualitative stories of teachers and students are central ingredients in this book.

Clarkson Community High School in Clarkson, Western Australia, uses Invitational Education as its framework for school improvement. Here's what Principal John Young wrote in personal communication on April 17, 2020:

Invitational Education has driven school reform at Clarkson Community High School.

It provides a coherent scaffold for systemic school improvement. The starfish analogy is easy to remember. The starfish motif is emblematic of a powerful synergy which is greater than the sum of the parts. The 5P's provide focus when analyzing challenges and developing new initiatives. Thomas Jones (2020), former Head of English Learning at Clarkson explains,

> The five domains exist in practically every environment and contribute to the success or failure of each individual. This involves the people, places, policies, programs and processes. There is now a strong case for the 5P's to occupy a more prominent place in our school leaders' thinking, as they forge a new reality where teachers work together innovatively to enhance student learning in a post pandemic world.

We have seen the benefits of our focus on Invitational Education at Clarkson. Students' literacy and numeracy outcomes trend upward to graduation. Student behaviour and engagement show documented improvement, too. Invitational Education provided a scaffolded approach to improving the social-emotional skills of our students and staff. The intentionality of our combined efforts has created a pervasively positive climate, which supports and involves all stakeholders in making the learning visible.

WHY INVITATIONAL EDUCATION?

These are challenging times for education, beyond the pressing demands for safe and healthy schools. In addition to the call for school safety, educators are pressured to do more, with less, and do it even better to attain high-stakes results in a time of great fear and uncertainty. As is often the case during times of great challenge, it is easy to lose sight of important educational goals and merely ask for a redoubling of effort. This frenzied pressure is taking its toll as more and more teachers express second thoughts about their vocational choice, counselors experience "compassion fatigue," principals report "disillusionment," and the general public sees "teacher wars" (Goldstein, 2014) and the vilification of public schooling.

A particularly destructive element that began in the 1980s is high-stakes standardized testing. As Sally Butzin, developer of the Project CHILD instructional system, commented in a personal communication, "The problem with standardized tests is that kids are not standardized." In her book *Creating Joyful Classrooms* (2018), Butzin points out the major drawbacks of high-stakes testing, particularly in elementary schools. Schools in and for a democratic society recognize, along with John Dewey (1916/1966), that each individual is a unique and important part of many vital groups. To attempt to standardize children in schools is to dishonor their uniqueness and their communities.

Invitational Education redirects the energy of current challenges to teaching, learning, leading, and schooling by reconnecting with the deeper hopes of educators.

Anya Kamenetz (2015) describes the frustration of teachers and parents in *The Test: Why Our Schools Are Obsessed with Standardized Testing—But You Don't Have to Be*. In large and small schools and in communities of all sizes, educators and parents are complaining about the narrowing of the school curriculum and the demeaning of teachers. In response to concerns about tying student test scores to teacher evaluation, even past U.S. Secretary of Education Arne Duncan complained, "I believe testing issues today are sucking the oxygen out of the room in a whole lot of schools" (Bidwell, 2014).

The proper role of testing is for instruction and diagnostics that will lead to student learning of meaningful material. The improper role of testing is to hand out bonuses and incentives, punish principals, fire teachers, defeat superintendents, and close schools. This improper role narrows the curriculum, forces teachers to teach to the test, and often encourages cheating by students and teachers. Moreover, when tests are improperly used, schools are likely to eliminate or reduce subjects like poetry, history, music, fine arts, and physical education, which are not as likely to show up on tests. Clearly there is a need for a fresh and innovative approach to education. Therefore, we have introduced the concept of Invitational Education.

Invitational Education redirects the energy of current challenges to teaching, learning, leading, and schooling by reconnecting with the deeper hopes of educators, by heading educational practices in a justifiable and consistent direction, and by offering holistic strategies for handling difficult situations. To do this, a language that expresses care is essential.

Caring provides the basis for an ethical system that guides action to sustain the vital connections of human existence. Caring is reflected in the stance taken as caregivers address the needs of others. Invitational Education provides a language that expresses this caring stance and a practice that exhibits it.

A Language That Expresses Care

We speak with words;
but words are not just uttered,
they can be chosen.
We use a language;
but that language is not merely words,
It can be a unique way of choosing to be in the world.
We teach others a way of being in the world;
but they are not mere recipients,
they can also choose to share with us their lives and hopes.

—JMN

Teaching, learning, and leading involve delicate and precious relationships. The words used to describe these relational activities are not neutral, because words involve choices, perspectives, and hopes. These in turn affect what people see, think, and do. Unfortunately, educators have often used words and conceptual systems that violate the integrity of people and the educative process.

Many words used to describe teaching and leading are based on a "doing-to" relationship. Educators are directed to motivate, reinforce, build, shape, enhance, modify, and "turn on" others. As well intentioned as these directions may be, they are fundamentally misguided. People are not passive recipients who can be turned on and cranked out. They are active participants in the process of trying to construct a meaningful life. A "doing-to" language is ethically inappropriate for working with people. Done well from a metaphorical point of view, a "doing-with" relationship is more like dancing with a person than like stuffing olives. In teachers' lounges there is a feeling of success when a teacher can announce with a smile, "They were really with me today." That is one of the key responses of participating in a "doing-with" relationship and symbolizes that "We are all in it together."

The invitational metaphor "teaching as inviting" was developed in response to the treatment of students and teachers as functionaries. The corollary to the metaphor is that education is a "doing-with" relationship, teaching creatively calls forth participation in beneficial activities, and learning is fundamentally connected to a person's intrinsic motive to seek meaning in the world. As used here, an inviting message is a summary description of those signals—transmitted by people, places, policies, programs, or processes—that present something beneficial for consideration and acceptance. These 5 Ps will be introduced more fully throughout the book.

Inviting signals are intended to inform people that they

- are able, valuable, and responsible;
- have opportunities to participate in their personal and collective development; and
- are cordially summoned to take advantage of these opportunities.

Conversely, disinviting signals inform their recipients that they

- are irresponsible, incapable, and worthless;
- cannot meaningfully participate in activities of any significance; and
- are not personally offered opportunities to engage.

An inviting message is an effort to establish a cooperative interaction; a disinviting message is an effort to establish a controlling or negating interaction. Inviting and disinviting messages take countless forms and deal with all human relationships. People are surrounded by these messages, from formal requests to informal urgings, from verbal comments to nonverbal behaviors, from official policies

The Invitational metaphor "teaching as inviting" was developed in response to the treatment of students and teachers as functionaries.

and programs to unwritten rituals and agendas. Individually and collectively, these messages play a significant role in determining what happens in schools.

An inviting message may be as formal as a bronze pin presented at an awards program, a leadership role for a special project, a complimentary note sent to parents, or an email thanking people for their help. It may also be as informal as a teacher taking special notice of a child's new shoes, as subtle as providing a cough drop for a nagging cough, or as nonverbal as a smile, nod, pat, or wink. Even when we choose not to respond, for example several seconds of silence at the right moment ("wait-time") can be most inviting.

THE POWER OF THE INVITING PROCESS

Everything the teacher does as well as the manner in which he does it incites the child to respond in some way or another and each response tends to set the child's attitude in some way or another. (Dewey, 1933, p. 59)

Individuals have a basic need to be noticed and noticed favorably by others. As William James (1890) commented long ago, "No more fiendish punishment could be devised, were such a thing possible, than that one should be turned loose in society and remain absolutely unnoticed by all the members thereof" (p. 179). This basic need for affirmation has also been described by Martin Buber: "Man [*sic*] wishes to be confirmed in his being by man and wishes to have a presence in the being of the other . . . secretly and bashfully he watches for a Yes which allows him to be and which can come only from one human person to another. It is from one person to another that the heavenly bread of self-being is passed" (1965, p. 71). Thus, from James's and Buber's perspectives, individuals help create one another.

Following James's and Buber's thinking, it appears that no one is self-made. The process begins with adult caregivers. What children learn from parents is critical. When children are treated with respect, they learn to respect themselves. When they are treated with trust, they learn to trust themselves and others. When they are treated with warmth, they learn to care for themselves and others. When parents instill an appetite for learning, and hold definite expectations, the child is far more likely to excel at school. It is sad that so few parents practice parental warmth, respect, and definite expectations. Daniel Siegel and Tina Payne Bryson (2020) provide rich examples of how parents can develop a caring, optimistic, respectful, and trusting relationship with their children, even during challenging times.

More than 50 years ago, Joan Anglund (1964) wrote that childhood should be the "happy hour." Tragically, many children live a nightmare. They are psychologically crippled and pauperized by rejection, brutality, and general neglect. Some children are beaten down by significant people in their lives, much like the birch tree victims of ice storms. Although schools may never be able to right the children fully—everything that happens to a child happens forever—educators can make a profound and positive difference. Education is an imaginative act of hope.

Each day students are influenced by the way the school bus driver greets them as they step on the bus, by the policies established by the school board, by the way the food is prepared and served in the cafeteria. They are also influenced by the way the physical environment is maintained, by the way classes are conducted, and by the nature and availability of programs. Everything in the school counts, either positively or negatively. Simply ensuring that bathrooms are clean and well-stocked with paper can make students and adults feel more valued, while leaving them unattended sends an opposite message. We live in a binary system. Successful leaders are obsessed with making their school welcoming from top to bottom, inside and out.

Art Combs, a colleague, shared a beautiful analogy to illustrate that everything counts. Imagine that each adult in a school had only one thimbleful of milk for each student. When one teacher encounters a child who is on the point of starvation she thinks: "A thimbleful of milk won't help." So, she gives her thimbleful to another healthier child. However, if every adult in the school gives the emaciated child their thimbleful of milk, that child may survive. Every thimbleful of milk counts. This means that everyone in the school is a stakeholder. In an inviting school, everyone contributes and everyone benefits. This is both a clear responsibility and a beautiful opportunity.

The positive effect of consistently caring actions cannot be overlooked, especially in the most dire circumstances. Compelling research on the adverse effects of chronic trauma on a child's physical, social, and emotional well-being and brain development has inspired schools to provide Trauma-Informed Schools workshops for educators. The Center on the Developing Child at Harvard University ("Key Concepts: Toxic Stress," n.d.) provides extensive research-based findings on childhood trauma and the importance of consistent, caring, and dependable relationships with adults:

> **Toxic stress response** can occur when a child experiences strong, frequent, and/or prolonged adversity—such as physical or emotional abuse, chronic neglect, caregiver substance abuse or mental illness, exposure to violence, and/or the accumulated burdens of family economic hardship—without adequate adult support. This kind of prolonged activation of the stress response systems can disrupt the development of brain architecture and other organ systems, and increase the risk for stress-related disease and cognitive impairment, well into the adult years.
>
> When toxic stress response occurs continually, or is triggered by multiple sources, it can have a cumulative toll on an individual's physical and mental health—for a lifetime. The more adverse experiences in childhood, the greater the likelihood of developmental delays and later health problems, including heart disease, diabetes, substance abuse, and depression. Research also indicates that supportive, responsive relationships with caring adults as early in life as possible can prevent or reverse the damaging effects of toxic stress response.

Of all the things that count, nothing is as important as the people in the process. Whiteboards, tablets, computers, apps, and other technological advances may play an important role in education, but they cannot substitute for human relationships. Teaching is a way of being with people. This "being-with" process has a great impact on students' ideas about themselves and their abilities.

Even more than "being with," Invitational Education suggests a bidding to go somewhere, to see people not only as they are, but also as they might become, to look ahead to tomorrow's promise. In her book *Inviting Students to Learn* (2010), Jenny Edwards provides 100 tips for communicating effectively with our students. In the following examples, Edwards suggests using words about time combined with words that describe a perception or feeling, to help students realize that their perceptions about their abilities can change:

- "So *right now*, you *feel* that you don't yet know what to do."
- "So *at that time*, you *believed* that you couldn't do it." (p. 52)

Donna Jackson is an extraordinary principal of the Jackson Elementary School, located in Jonesboro, Georgia. The school is surrounded by poverty. Every day Donna asks her students, "What college are you planning to attend?" Students have learned to respond with a chosen college. Donna is planting seeds that will have a profound impact on the futures of her students. Most educators who have been in schools a while understand the importance of having a positive vision of the future.

> *Research also indicates that supportive, responsive relationships with caring adults as early in life as possible can prevent or reverse the damaging effects of toxic stress response.*

An elementary school teacher wrote,

> In my second grade class, I had each child express what he or she would like to be as an adult. After listening to each child, I said: "Everybody look up at your star in the sky and reach for it!" Every child in the room started reaching as high as possible. The amazing thing is that they all wanted to learn something each day just so I could say to them: "Reach up and see if you're a little bit closer to your star."

Each human watches closely for clues in the behavior of others. A teacher's verbal and nonverbal signals that the student is able, valuable, and responsible can be marvelously reassuring to a child struggling with a difficult spelling word, a complex math problem, a threatening oral report, or an effort to reach a star. Successful teachers realize that humans are in a constant process of being created. They use this realization to develop appropriate and caring patterns of communication.

PATTERNS OF COMMUNICATION

Inviting the development of human potential is a simple concept, but it can be a highly complex activity. Even the smallest and subtlest experience can have a profound impact. Life's whispered invitations are often intangible, and they can be so subtle and indirect that individuals are sometimes unaware of their effects. A certain pattern exists, however, in the endless variety of messages transmitted in and around schools. When this pattern is brought into focus, previously unexamined factors can be identified that result in students feeling invited or disinvited in school.

Louis, a New York high school student, was particularly perceptive about how teachers' words and actions influenced what he believed to be true about his ability to succeed in their classes:

> If my teacher starts to sneer or if I do something wrong, like I answer a question wrong and she rolls her eyes, I take that as "I can't do this class." If you ask a question and the teacher says, "Oh come on, we went over that already," or "Enough questions, Louis, just try to pay attention," after several of those, you're not asking questions anymore.
>
> Although the teacher is just getting frustrated from the day, and not meaning to take it out on the kid, the kid no longer wants to try in school. It doesn't seem like a big deal to a teacher, but to a kid, it can make it seem like you actually hate the kid. That's not true, but we're kids and we think that. We're fragile—we're not adults yet. We're still learning.

FEELING INVITED

During the past 4 decades, thousands of students at various academic levels have provided the authors with examples of inviting or disinviting messages they received during their years of schooling. The great majority of students of various ages remember clearly what it was like to feel invited in school. Their illustrations fell into one of three categories: (1) able, (2) valuable, and (3) responsible. Feeling able, valuable, and responsible was beautifully expressed by a former student at Creative Primary School in Hong Kong, a model for Invitational Education. "I learned who I really am, and that I have gifts that will make me unique and this helped me survive in a high-pressured secondary school environment."

While the inviting approach is far more than verbal comments, below are examples of statements students remembered years after they were spoken.

Able:

- "Mr. Mac said I had made the most progress of anyone in the class."
- "I remember my science teacher saying I was a careful researcher."
- "My teacher asked me if she could take a copy of my paper to show at a teacher workshop."
- "My school counselor told me that I would 'flourish in AP Biology.'"
- "Even though I had only been teaching a few years, my supervisor encouraged me to get my administrative degree."

Valuable:

- "Mr. Evans cared enough to come to school a half hour early each morning just to help me with science."
- "My chorus teacher really cared what we had to say, and that's what most kids need. If we had a question, she wanted to hear about it. She pushed us to want to push ourselves."
- "The first day of school the secretary in the guidance office said she was going to teach me how to smile, and she did."
- "Even though there were a thousand kids in the school, the custodian always remembered my name."
- "The Superintendent told me I was the kind of teacher he wished his daughter could have."

Responsible:

- "Coach asked me to take the equipment out and explain the rules."
- "I'll never forget my teacher thanking me for going 'above and beyond' every day."
- "She didn't try to force us to work, but she made it clear that we would hurt ourselves by goofing off."
- "I remember my 3rd-grade teacher telling me how proud she was of our behavior during her absence—she said we were like 6th-graders!"
- "I was kind of a mess in middle school. Most teachers never gave me anything important to do. I guess they felt that they couldn't count on me. Mrs. Wilson was different. She always asked me to lead a reading group."

Again, and again, students reported that certain teachers had a flair for inviting. They felt that their teachers were partners in learning. One student wrote, "Whenever I was in Miss Penn's English class, I could feel myself becoming more intelligent!"

Louis, our perceptive New York student explains,

> When I find a teacher that believes in me, that pushes me and sees me as a person making my own decisions rather than just a kid on a track, I feel like I'm getting more respect. It makes me look forward to that class. I feel like that class is easier because now I have the teacher on my side. I'm not tackling my homework and tests on my own. That makes a huge difference.

In light of these comments it is not surprising that students learn best when placed in the care of educators who invite them to see themselves as able, valuable, and responsible and to behave accordingly.

Unfortunately, many students describe memories of their schooling that center on feelings of being worthless, incapable, and irresponsible. When asked to describe the messages they received in school, these students reported feelings of being disinvited.

FEELING DISINVITED

Many students explained that they felt disinvited in school simply because they were consistently overlooked. A likely name for these students would be "The Woodwork Kids." They simply fade into the woodwork. Sometimes this lack of presence can be a defense against bullying or undue pressure to excel. These students said they were seldom encouraged to participate in school activities, that they rarely played on a team, belonged to a club, held an office, attended a school function, or were even called on in class. They stated that they did not feel a part of school and that they seldom related with faculty and staff in even the most casual way. Their teachers usually returned papers without comment except for a letter grade, and they rarely seemed to notice the students' absences from school. These students suffered from a "caring disability"; not enough educators cared to invite them to participate in school life.

Adding to the problem of indifferent treatment, students who constantly feel disinvited may become defiant or decide to seek revenge. Most students are acutely aware when some are given more opportunities and encouragement than others. They feel there's a party going on and they haven't been invited. Those who feel disinvited remember keenly the slights they receive. The distinction between "disinvited" and "uninvited" can be seen in this example: If I say I am going to have a party and tell you that you are not invited, that's disinvited. If I have a party and don't invite you, that's uninvited.

Many students are disinvited by educators who, either intentionally or unintentionally, behave in ways that result in student embarrassment, frustration, and failure. A high school girl wrote,

> My Latin teacher did not like females, particularly "socially oriented" ones. And I met both requirements. I was in a room with my best friends, which included males and females. The teacher would pick me out and have me go to the board and write something in Latin. Of course, when I missed something, which was often, the entire class got a lecture on studying more and socializing less. But I had to stand in front of the class by myself the entire time while the lecture on the evils of "socializing" was being presented. I was usually so embarrassed I would end up crying in the bathroom where no one could see me.

More than 40 years ago, Canfield and Wells (1976) used the term *killer statements* to describe the means by which a student's feelings, thoughts, and creativity are "killed off" by another person's negative comments, physical gestures, or other behaviors. Novelist Laura Esquivel (1992) referred to these individuals as "frigid breath" people. Their very presence can dash optimism and hope, and their actions can be lethal. These actions may be little more than a teacher's suddenly stiffened spine when a child of another race touches his or her arm—or as elusive as the failure to call on or even look at certain children. A child's feelings of being disinvited, are described by Dick Gregory in his autobiography (1964):

> The teacher thought I was a troublemaker. All she saw from the front of the room was a little black boy who squirmed in his idiot's seat and made noises and poked the kids around him. I guess she couldn't see a kid who made noises because he wanted someone to know he was there. (p. 30)

Whether intentional or unintentional, disinviting messages can have long-lasting effects.

Students (and adults) who reported that they felt disinvited in school described experiences that could be divided into three categories of self-perception: (1) unable, (2) worthless, and (3) irresponsible. Here are some examples. Again, disinviting messages are received through more than verbal comments.

Unable:

- "A teacher told my mother, 'Your child will only be average.'"
- "My math teacher said, 'I don't understand why you don't get this.'"
- "My high school guidance counselor told me I'd better keep my job at McDonalds."
- "A teacher asked me why I couldn't follow simple directions."
- "My undergraduate professor told me, 'You'll never make it as a Math teacher. You should consider changing your major.'"

Worthless

- "On the first day of school, the teacher came in and said he wasn't supposed to teach this basic class, but that he was stuck with us."
- "The teacher said 'That's crazy! What's the matter with you?' His negative attitude toward me stood out like a bump on your nose."
- "I transferred to a new school after the year had started. When I appeared at the teacher's doorway, she said 'Oh, no, not another one!'"
- "My teacher told me I was the worst kid she ever taught."
- "My principal told me, 'Special education teachers are a dime-a-dozen.'"

Irresponsible:

- "The teacher said I had to be watched every minute."
- "She said I was worse than my brother, and I don't even have a brother."
- "Because I failed to bring my homework, the teacher asked me why I bothered coming to school."
- "She told the class we were discipline problems and were not to be trusted."
- "The coach told me he couldn't count on me for anything important."

As explained earlier, negative experiences may spur someone to future success, but this is likely to be true only of students who do not easily accept rejection and failure. Students who fight back against disinviting experiences do so only because they have a history of invitations received, accepted, and successfully acted upon. They have built up a partial immunity to failure. Students who readily accept disinviting messages about themselves and their abilities are usually those who have been infected with failure early in life. As one student wrote, "Hell, how can I feel good about myself when I'm stuck in the dummy class year after year?"

Research by Roderick (1994) demonstrates the impact of early failure on later school performance. She reported that students who are forced to repeat a grade from kindergarten to 6th grade are far more likely to drop out of school later even when differences in background and post-retention grades are controlled. Being retained and thus being over-age for a grade during adolescence may explain the higher dropout rate for failed students. Twenty years later David Berliner and Gene Glass (2014) reviewed the massive amount of empirical data on student retention and concluded that retaining students is almost always ineffective and often biased and mean-spirited. Not a pretty picture for institutions that are supposed to develop human potential.

> It seems clear that student success or failure is related to the ways in which students perceive themselves and their environments—and that these perceptions are influenced by the prevailing nature of the messages they receive in school.

The picture drawn from countless descriptions is that students live in a world of attitudes, expectancies, and evaluations. The full impact of this world has yet to be determined, but it seems clear that student success or failure is related to the ways in which students perceive themselves and their environments—and that these perceptions are influenced by the prevailing nature of the messages they receive in school. Creating, sustaining, and enhancing truly inviting schools are no guarantee that students' perceptions of themselves will be enhanced. School experiences are only part of the environment. Children come from rural, suburban, urban, wealthy, and poor areas. If a child comes from a negating home environment and enters a truly inviting school, that child might survive. If a child comes from a warm and supportive home environment and enters a negating school, that child might survive. But if a child comes from a negating home environment and enters a negating school environment, there is a guarantee that the child will develop a negative view of him- or herself, others, and the world.

SUMMARY

This opening chapter addresses the critical need to intentionally work with the ongoing patterns of communication to move beyond physical safety in schools and consider the deeper social and emotional worlds in which children live. Invitational Education serves as a vehicle for understanding the continual influence of people, places, policies, programs, and processes on students (and all other stakeholders, as well). Some students are invited to learn, some are overlooked, and some are dissuaded. These memories can be retained for many years, as the statements from students demonstrated. Practice-based evidence shared in Chapter 8 indicates that students respond best when they share the company of educators who believe them to be able, valuable, and responsible, and who intentionally summon them to share in these beliefs. This is an important approach to schooling in and for a democratic society.

Chapter 2 offers a detailed look at the foundations of Invitational Education, the theoretical and practical grounding for developing a theory of intentional practice for developing inviting schools.

FURTHER REFLECTIONS AND ACTIVITIES

At the end of each chapter we offer questions for reflection and discussion, as well as some suggested activities. Creating buy-in for anything new in education is typically met with a skeptical response such as, "Here we go again! Here comes another new thing on our already full plate." Educators have been given so many new curricula to implement and strategies to try, many become defensive or even anxious at the thought of something else new. Some have learned to smile and look enthusiastic at the introductory meeting, only to walk out into the parking lot and say, "This too will get shelved in a few months, so I'm not going to waste my time learning about it."

The refreshing thing about Invitational Education is that it is not a program. It is not a series of carefully worded objectives that you will be evaluated on. It is simply a way of thinking about and experimenting with how everything we do and how we do it sends a message. So, as you give thought to using Invitational Education as your framework for school improvement, the best advice we can give you is to go slow, keep the buy-in door open, and don't judge others along the way. Some people will jump onboard right away. Others will feel uncomfortable with the ideas and assume that in the eyes of others they are part of the problem. In addition to explaining what it is and how it might benefit your school, try sharing how it is making you rethink some of the things you habitually say or do—sharing your realization that, at times, others may very well find your words or actions to be judgmental, dismissive, or controlling. Telling people what you are learning about yourself and how you plan to communicate differently will open many minds and reduce defensive responses.

As an educator, it is essential that you communicate that you personally have something to learn from this and that you would like to improve. Those who don't often find that a segment of a school will respond by saying to their colleagues, "It's all very interesting. I'll wait to see if those promoting this are going to practice what they're preaching." Encourage others to read with you and share their thoughts. Soon after, you'll discover a group of people who may not raise their hand at a staff meeting to express interest but will catch up with you privately to encourage you to move forward. Be willing to work with the volunteers and be sure to include all staff in the introduction and exploration from the very beginning. Avoid judging or pressuring the people who stay on the sidelines. Spend time with your biggest critics. Learn what's important to them and try to incorporate that in the school's initiatives. When you begin working on something that resonates with them, you'll find your biggest supporters.

Questions for personal reflection and a favorite activity for a faculty meeting discussion about Invitational Education:

1. How does an invitational framework address the root causes of educator and student stress and violence in today's schools?
2. What are some of the benefits of replacing "doing to" punitive disciplinary approaches with "doing with" invitational approaches?
3. Staff Meeting Activity: The following reflective exercise works well with a group of people. You will need two different colors of sticky notes, preferably blue and orange. After completing the exercise, participants may enjoy reading the article "An Introduction to the Metaphor of Blue and Orange Cards" (2010), which is included in Appendix E.

Instructions: "Think about a very positive (inviting) comment a teacher said to you or about you in the past. It might be from 1st grade or your college years. Write it on a blue sticky note. Now try to recall a very negative (disinviting) comment a teacher said to or about you. Write it on an orange sticky note." (Provide time for reflection and writing.)

Now invite a few volunteers to share a "blue" or "orange" comment with the group and identify how they perceived the comment. "Did you take it as a comment about your ability, value, or responsibility?" Each comment should fit in one or more of these three categories.

As the receiver of the message, it is how you perceive it that is most important to consider. Allow participants time to reflect on their experience without interruption.

Before the meeting, place three large pieces of chart paper on a wall in the meeting room. Write one of these words on the top of each piece of paper: Able, Valuable, Responsible. After a few people have had time to share their memories and their colleagues have commented as they wish, ask all the participants to post their positive and negative notes on the charts on the wall. Instruct them to place their notes under the category that best describes how *they* received this message.

Allow time for the group to do a "gallery walk" by standing silently in front of the charts and reflecting on the many positive and negative messages that their colleagues have received throughout their lives. Some will comment on how they might have interpreted the message differently and placed it on a different chart. This provides an opportunity to consider that we all may interpret the same message differently. Provide more opportunity for reflection by hanging the charts in the staff room or recording the comments on a document that can be distributed to the staff for further reflection and discussion.

Foundations of Invitational Education

> Human behavior is always a product of how people see themselves and the situations in which they are involved. Although this fact seems obvious, the failure of people everywhere to comprehend it is responsible for much of human misunderstanding, maladjustment, conflict and loneliness. (Combs et al., 1978, p. 15)

Any structure needs a solid and flexible foundation to ensure a stable and workable framework. For example, a bridge without a firm and adaptable grounding is a dangerous route to travel on. If its foundation is too rigid any movement is the beginning of its faltering. If its foundation is too flexible it gets blown in whatever direction the wind is blowing. The key concepts and strategies of Invitational Education are built upon three interlocking and growing foundations: the democratic ethos, the perceptual tradition, and self-concept theory. Each of these robust foundations provides the basis for implementing and sustaining social and emotional safety in schools. Without a firm grasp of these foundations, the reason for some suggested practices that follow will elude a coherent rationale and will be difficult to sustain.

DEMOCRATIC ETHOS

The democratic ethos lies at the base of the foundations of Invitational Education. The other foundations—the use of the perceptual tradition to understand people and self-concept theory to focus on the uniqueness of individuals—are built on the primacy of a commitment to the idea that everyone matters. With this in mind, the inviting approach is a part of a larger ethical project that attempts to call forth the possibilities of people leading more fulfilling lives. This deep-seated ethical commitment enables Invitational Education to go beyond the fad-of-the-month programs that are incessantly thrown at educators and to focus on what really matters: people and their potential to lead fulfilling lives.

And so, the heart of creating and maintaining a positive social and emotional environment is not a series of techniques for getting students to perform better on high-stakes tests, although it often has that effect. It is not a way to get people to feel good about themselves no matter what they do, although it has a self-concept focus that emphasizes the importance of positive and realistic self-talk. It is not a public relations wake-up call to get people mobilized to talk to the media about the good things that are happening in their school, although it can certainly help organize such efforts. Rather, the inviting approach is rooted in a much larger ethical project. It is rooted in the aim of enabling people to live more fulfilling lives through positive, non-coercive means by being involved in doing-with relationships. Deep down, a commitment to creating a socially and emotionally safe place for people in schools is a commitment to the basic notion that all people matter. Individuals and communities have a need and a right to participate in deciding the principles, policies, and practices that guide their lives. This is a deep sense of the concept of democracy that goes beyond the customary conventions of voting for representatives in public elections and forming and participating in political parties.

> *The inviting approach is rooted in a much larger ethical project. It is rooted in the aim of enabling people to live more fulfilling lives through positive, non-coercive means by being involved in doing-with relationships.*

Important as these conventions can be, they are only one way of putting into practice the fruitful ideal that everyone matters. The democratic ethos, however, runs much deeper, not only in theory but in practice. It connects to the importance of attending to the communication of messages that call forth the human potential to live educational lives. This communicative sense of democracy has been an important concept for educators for more than a century. John Dewey emphasized the critical significance of communication in *Democracy and Education* (1916/1966): "*A democracy is more than a form of government; it is primarily a mode of associated living, of conjoint communicated experiences*" (p. 87). For Dewey, it is through the communication process that people can develop and maintain common values and enjoy community living. Mutual respect is a hallmark of this commitment to a life of dialogue that involves working with people in doing-with as opposed to doing-to ways. In addition, Dewey emphasized a commitment to democracy because it is the most educative form of governance. As people work to understand others, make their own thoughts public, and cooperate to create, implement, and evaluate imaginative approaches to shared problems, they grow personally, socially, and emotionally. This then can carry on to other parts of their life. A century later, Martha Nussbaum (2010) pointed out that without a commitment to understanding the complex issues of a pluralistic world and a commitment to understanding the perspectives of diverse people, our shared way of life will be shattered and human capabilities for leading fulfilling lives will be greatly limited.

Democratic practices are founded on open and free dialogue that promotes social responsibility. As people communicate in a pluralistic society, they deal with an endless variety of individual perceptual worlds, unique self-concepts, and diverse cultural traditions. This requires social intelligence, which is the ability to use a variety of perspectives, to see things from the viewpoint of others, and to deal with the complexities and challenges of democratic living. The development of social intelligence leads to a stronger sense of collective responsibility—a sense and ideal that all are in it together.

Used as a guiding ideal, the democratic ethos points to ever-enriching communicative process. As such an ideal, the democratic ethos should not be judged as a waste of time or a distraction because it is not attained in every, or even most, instances. Rather, ideals, as Robert Nozick (1989) indicated, should be judged on the basis of whether they enable people to attain more of what they consider to be of worth. A commitment to the democratic ethos is therefore a commitment to the conditions and processes that make understanding, mutual respect, and continuous dialogue possible. Thus, a commitment to democratic practice and social justice is essential to establishing safe and successful schools. For this communicative sense of democracy to work better, a theoretical perspective that shows respect for the person is necessary. The perceptual tradition fits that bill. It links the expansive nature of democracy with the intentional importance of paying attention to how people see themselves and the situations they are in.

THE PERCEPTUAL TRADITION

The starting point is the notion that each person is a conscious agent: They experience, interpret, construct, decide, act, and are ultimately responsible for their actions.

If every person matters, then it is important to have a viewpoint that builds on the perspective of the person. Invitational Education has its roots in the perceptual approach to understanding human behavior. Rather than viewing people as objects to be shaped, reinforced, and conditioned, or as captives of unconscious urges or unfulfilled desires, or as computational machines that can only make binary choices, the perceptual tradition views people as they typically see themselves, others, and the world. The starting point is the notion that each person is a conscious agent: They experience, interpret, construct, decide, act, and are ultimately responsible for their actions.

Historically and recently, many philosophers and psychologists have contributed to the perceptual approach. The long list includes the following:

- William James's description of consciousness (1890)
- George Herbert Mead's perspective on the social nature of perception (1934)
- Prescott Lecky's notion of the consistent nature of perceptions (1945)
- George Kelly's development of personal constructs as the basis of perceptions (1955)
- Gordon Allport's (1955, 1961) and Carl Rogers's (1947, 1951, 1969, 1974, 1980) career-long emphases on people as perceptive, purposeful, and capable of taking responsibility for their present lives and future aspirations
- Sidney Jourard's use of the concept of self-disclosure (1968, 1971)
- William Powers's connection of perception and systems theory (1973)
- Martin Seligman's explanation of learned helplessness (1975) and learned optimism (2006)
- Donald Meichenbaum's cognitive behavior modification (1977)
- Robert Kegan's exploration of the evolving nature of meaning-making and perception (1982)
- Walter Truett Anderson's (1990) description of postmodern beliefs and behavior
- Albert Bandura's social cognitive theory (2012)
- Dan Siegel's (2007, 2018) description of interpersonal neurobiology, internal attunement, and mindful reflection
- John Hattie's (2017) updated list of factors influencing student achievement
- Antonio Damasio's (2018) extensive work on feelings, emotions, and social life

Invitational Education builds on the perceptual tradition and places special emphasis on the Snygg-Combs theory of perception. First presented in 1949 by Donald Snygg and Arthur Combs, this theory has been revised numerous times and applied to various fields of endeavor. The basic contention of this theory is that people behave according to how they see themselves and the situations in which they are involved (Combs, Avila, & Purkey, 1978). Because of this emphasis on understanding and working with people as they normally see themselves and the world, perceptual theory seems well suited for creating a safe environment in many professional settings, including teaching, administering, counseling, nursing, leading, and related human service activities.

Four hallmarks of the perceptual tradition follow, along with examples of how they support Invitational Education.

Behavior Is Based on Perceptions

The perceptual tradition seeks to explain why people do the things they do by postulating that human behavior is determined by, and pertinent to, the phenomenal field of the experiencing person at the moment of acting. In other words, each individual behaves according to how the world appears at that instant. From this vantage point, there is no such thing as illogical behavior—every person is behaving in the way that makes the most sense to her or him at that particular instant. What may seem illogical from an external point of view, and even upon reflection from an internal viewpoint, is only an inadequate understanding of what the world looks like from the internal viewpoint of the behaving person at the moment of action.

What may seem illogical from an external point of view, and even upon reflection from an internal viewpoint, is only an inadequate understanding of what the world looks like from the internal viewpoint of the behaving person at the moment of action.

Perhaps a personal example can clarify this. Several years ago, one of the authors of this book was trying to learn to hang glide. He had soloed an airplane and knew the basic rule of aerodynamics: "Thou shalt always maintain thy airspeed or thou shalt smite the ground." However, when he was taking his first "easy" flight in a hang glider that was not designed to take him more than five feet off the ground, he got caught by an updraft and was suddenly 35 feet high. At that moment, rather than leveling off as he had been taught, he closed his eyes and pushed the frame of the kite away from his body and promptly climbed to 60 feet! Somehow, through a series of fortunate events, he returned to earth without being killed.

Why did he close his eyes and push the frame forward when he knew the consequences of such an action? There are various explanations for his behavior, each with its defenders. A behaviorist might conclude that he had been insufficiently reinforced in the standard way of leveling the frame and thus had not been properly conditioned to emit the correct response. A Freudian might hypothesize that perhaps he had an unconscious death wish and that his behavior was a manifestation of this basic impulse. A computational analyst might conclude that he had not arranged his possible actions in a logical order. A perceptualist, by comparison, would try to "read behavior backwards," to discover what the world looked like to the student pilot the moment he closed his eyes and pushed the frame forward. In looking back at the incident, the novice was totally surprised to be up so high so soon. At that moment, he could think of nothing else but to do the safest thing he could—to close his eyes and get the frame as far away from himself as fast as possible. His reasoning then was, "If I can't see the ground, it can't hurt me." Later, such thinking seemed absurd. At the instant of behaving, however, closing his eyes and pushing away the frame made the most sense. Threat narrows perception and reduces differentiations.

As used here, perception refers to the differentiations a person is able to make in his or her personal world of experience. In the hang glider example, the threatened person had a severely restricted perceptual field called tunnel vision (Combs et al., 1978). Tunnel vision is triggered by real or imagined threat. Because of threat, and thus a restricted perceptual field, he could make only limited differentiations.

As further evidence of the power of perception, alcohol consumption appears to be used by social drinkers and alcoholics alike to reduce perceptions of personal failure (Hull & Young, 1993). As Taylor (1989) pointed out, clarity can be quite painful at times.

The perceptual tradition holds that to understand human behavior you must make sense of how things appear from the vantage point of the individual perceiver at the moment of behaving. From the perceptual point of view, the fundamental unit of analysis is the way an experiencing human being views self, others, and the world at a particular moment in time.

The perceptual tradition implies that although there is much more to the world than what is presently perceived, it takes a disciplined effort to move beyond one's initial perceptions. This has been well documented by Gardner (1991, 1999, 2011) and Kahneman (2011), who have shown that people lock into perceptions developed early in life and those agreed upon by people around them. These fast, intuitive perceptions are a necessity of life but can block out more complex processes of the world, processes that can be understood by slower, sustained disciplined inquiry.

Fortunately, each person's perceptual field can be continually enriched, expanded, and modified. The ideas that individuals can enhance their perceptions and that their perceptual fields are capable of incalculable expansion and modification serve as major reasons for Invitational Education. Gabriel Garcia Marquez, in his classic book *Love in the Time of Cholera* (1988), expressed the concept of constant renewal:

> He allowed himself to be swayed by his conviction that human beings are not born once and for all on the day their mothers gave birth to them. But that life obliges them over and over again to give birth to themselves. (p. 165)

Without such a belief in human development, Invitational Education would be very limited. Such a belief provides something to continually appreciate and reach for: a coming together for creative, worthwhile purposes that can extend the quality of human experiences.

Perceptions Are Learned

No one reading these words was born with the perceptions they presently possess. Perceptions change over time. Through myriad encounters with the world, particularly those with significant others, people develop certain fundamental perceptions that serve as organizing filters for making sense of the world. Without such a

Thus, any change in perceptions alters one's view of the past, present, future, and the imaginable.

filtering system, each person would be relentlessly bombarded by unrelated stimuli, creating an infinitely chaotic existence. Without an organizing "in here," there could be no organized "out there."

Perceptions Shape Behavior

Perceptions influence the memories people use to understand the present and anticipate the future. For example, imagine someone hands you a box and says there is a snake in it. If you fear snakes, you will respond in a certain way whether or not there is a snake in the box. In addition, perceptions affect the possibilities that people can imagine and the goals that they are willing to work for. Thus, any change in perceptions alters one's view of the past, present, future, and the imaginable.

Invitational Education is based on an understanding of and respect for people's perceptual worlds. These perceptual worlds are not to be taken lightly, for they provide the basis for meaning and behavior. How sensitive educators are to how people perceive themselves, others, and the world affects the messages they choose to extend and accept. Fortunately, sensitivity to the perceptual worlds of oneself and others can be enhanced through reflection.

Perceptions Can Be Reflected Upon

The ability to examine one's perceptions is essential to Invitational Education. Being aware of past and present perceptions and being able and willing to go beyond them permit the development of a deeper level of understanding of self, others, and the world. As Csikszentmihalyi (2014) points out, reflection can lead a person to develop a more differentiated and integrated self, that is, a personality with many interests creatively harmonized.

Reflection also provides a basis for hope because there is no inevitable future as long as people are willing to rethink perceptions of the past and apply this thinking to different aspects of their lives. Although people cannot change the past, they can change their perceptions of previous events and consequently open more possibilities in the future. For this to work, it is important to savor present perceptions and imaginatively project

these perceptions, and the means of their attainment, into the future. This then extends to the importance of developing reflected perceptions about the perceptual process. These reflected perceptions, or meta-perceptions, enable individuals to understand the perspectival nature of his or her personal view of situations, people, and possibilities.

> *Reflection also provides a basis for hope because there is no inevitable future as long as people are willing to rethink perceptions of the past and apply this thinking to different aspects of their lives.*

Mindfulness practices, now commonly used in schools, have brought perceptual reflection to the forefront of well-being. Segal, Williams, and Teasdale (2002) explain that mindfulness teaches us to simply acknowledge our thoughts and emotions, "without immediately being hooked into automatic tendencies to judge, fix, or want things to be other than they are."

Mindful breathing is a tool for tuning into our experience, body, and emotions, by simply noticing them without reacting. Dan Siegel, clinical psychologist and codirector of the UCLA Mindful Awareness Research Center, has contributed extensively to the relatively new field of interpersonal neurobiology. He explains (2010) how the integration of three parts of our brain comprise the basis of our well-being. When we have a strong thought or emotion, the amygdala (responsible for fight, flight, and freeze responses) takes control and disengages from both the prefrontal cortex (responsible for nine functions, including response flexibility, fear modulation, empathy, and insight) as well as the hippocampus (where information and memory is stored.) While the amygdala is "in charge," we may react rather than beneficially respond. Mindful breathing gives us time to quiet the amygdala and reconnect it with the thinking and memory parts of the brain. It helps us put space between a strong stimulus and our response. Simple mindful practices are helping both students and educators to reduce stress by intentionally pausing and reflecting, in order to calm the mind and make more beneficial choices of behavior.

With an understanding that all perceptions are always from some vantage point, a certain humility and ambition ensues: humility, because with the understanding that all perceptions are limited we have the realization that we never possess the complete picture; ambition, because it is possible to develop new and better ways to perceive things. Like it or not, each person is not a neutral observer in a predetermined reality. Rather, from the perceptual point of view, each person is an active participant in the construction of their reality.

This section thus far has emphasized that people behave according to how they perceive themselves, others, and the world; that these perceptions are learned; and that they can be reflected upon. Now, please consider what is a vital perception for each individual: perception of oneself.

SELF-CONCEPT THEORY

Of all the perceptions people learn, none seems to affect one's search for personal significance and identity more than self-perception—one's view of who one is and how one fits in the world. This section on self-concept theory is the largest and most detailed of the three foundations because it deals most directly with the fragile and delicate feelings and emotions of real people in real situations in and out of schools.

Some theorists (Combs et al., 1978; Rogers, 1951, 1967) have postulated that the maintenance, protection, and enhancement of the perceived self (one's own personal existence as viewed by oneself) is the basic motive behind all human behavior. Use of this basic notion, organized into what is generally known as self-concept theory, can clarify and integrate seemingly unrelated aspects of life in classrooms. For example, students who have learned to see themselves as troublemakers may respond by being discipline problems, just as students who have learned to view themselves as scholars may spend many hours in libraries. The dynamics are the same, even if the resulting behaviors are quite different.

Recent research supports a positive and important relationship between self-concept and academic achievement. John Hattie (2017) incorporated the results of 1200 meta-analyses in his updated list of factors that impact student learning. Included in the list of factors with very high impact are "student self-efficacy," with an effect size of .92, and "student motivation and approach," with an effect size of .69. Even more notable is "teacher estimates of student achievement" as having the *highest impact influence*, with an effect size of 1.62. Understanding self-concept, the influence of teacher mindset on student achievement, and its direct relation to Invitational Education is advantageous for educators who wish to function in a professionally inviting manner.

In his book *Visible Learning* (2009), Hattie referred to Invitational Education as "invitational learning theory," noting the significant effect of a safe and caring classroom environment on student learning: "This is not "niceness" at work, but an approach that places much reliance on the teachers and schools to make learning exciting, engaging, and enduring. Where there are school differences, it is these types of effects that are the most powerful" (p. 34).

Self-concept has served as a central part of many human personality theories and the basis for numerous programs in education. The emerging literature is so vast that this chapter can examine only four aspects of self-concept that relate most directly to Invitational Education: (1) self-concept development, (2) the symmetry of the self, (3) self-concept as a guidance system, and (4) the significance of positive self-regard.

Self-Concept Development

No one is born with a self-concept. The development and structure of self-awareness is a lifelong research project. The ever-widening experiences of the developing person constantly modify the self-concept. By experiencing the world through inviting and disinviting interactions with others, as well as through interactions with oneself, the developing person organizes a theory of personal existence.

Each person learns early to identify with categories (for example, female, African American, Southerner, Canadian, Methodist, Virginian, and so forth) and with attributes (for example, good/bad, strong/weak, valuable/worthless, responsible/irresponsible, able/unable, and so on). Harter (1983, 1988) proposed that self-concept consists of domains that differ in significance according to an individual's age. Some domains are more significant at certain ages than others. For example, job performance, social competence, and appearance are self-concept components that are salient factors in defining the self in adulthood.

Through countless interactions with the world, each individual gradually forges a self-concept, complete with a complex hierarchy of attributes and categories.

Through countless interactions with the world, each individual gradually forges a self-concept, complete with a complex hierarchy of attributes and categories. Marsh (1993) developed a schema that divides self-concept into components, including academic self-concept and social self-concept. In addition, he studied math self-concept and school self-concept.

The Symmetry of the Self

A person's self-concept is not simply a hodgepodge of cognitions and feelings. It has its own symmetry, characterized by stability, orderliness, balance, and harmony. This symmetry consists of two forces, the "I" and the "me" characteristics and attributes. The "I" represents immediate awareness. It is the very center of an individual's perceived existence. Examples would be "I am hungry" or "I am an American" or "I am angry."

Surrounding the "I" are myriad "me" characteristics and attributes. Each has its own influence, large or small, good or bad, healthy or unhealthy. These "me" characteristics and attributes can be categories (Baptist, father, lover) and characteristics (pretty, smart, ugly). The "me" characteristics and attributes are both mirrors for the "I" and a lens that filters the perceived world. Sometimes these "me" characteristics and attributes have an uneasy relationship with one another, especially when there is cognitive dissonance: "I'm Catholic, and I use birth control."

Because a person's self-concept is constructed through life experiences, it can be taught. This fact makes Invitational Theory indispensable. To simplify:

- The "I" constantly seeks to maintain, protect, and enhance itself.
- The "I" is the self-as-doer, the subject. The "me" characteristics and attributes are the self-as-object.
- The "I" seeks stability and resists change.
- The "me" characteristics and attributes serve as both a looking glass for the "I" and a lens for perceiving the world.
- Together, the "I" and "me" characteristics and attributes determine all human actions.
- The closer a "me" is to the "I," the more influence it has on behavior.
- A person's self-concept is constructed, therefore it can be taught.

Imagine the self-concept as a spiral, with the "I" in the center as in Figure 2.1. Notice the me characteristics and attributes closest to the "I" have the most influence, for they "have the king's ear." For example, "Me" as mother has far greater voice than "me" as golfer. Now, imagine the spiral in Figure 2.1 as a lake. This lake is constantly fed by a river of experience, good or bad, that flows into the lake at one end and exits at the other. The potential "me" characteristics and attributes can flow into the lake rapidly or slowly depending on what the world offers.

In the healthy personality, the river dependably provides the lake with a number of new "me" characteristics and attributes, mostly positive. For example, "I am now a college graduate." Likewise, old "me" characteristics and attributes are discarded and flow out of the lake: "I am no longer a student."

If too many negative characteristics and attributes enter the self (I am dumb, I am unwanted, I am unfit) it becomes flooded or drained, unpredictable, and provides little protection against the vicissitudes of life. When too many "me" characteristics and attributes strive for attention, or there is too much conflict, the "I" can lose self-direction and integrity. When there are too few "me" characteristics and attributes, the individual begins to lose his or her identify and even his or her perceived existence ("I don't know who I am").

To complicate things further, potential new "me" characteristics and attributes can be accepted or rejected depending on what is already inside the self-concept. For example, if a student thinks he is stupid, and the teacher tells him he is smart, it is very likely the teacher's comment will be rejected.

Figure 2.1. The Symmetry of the Self

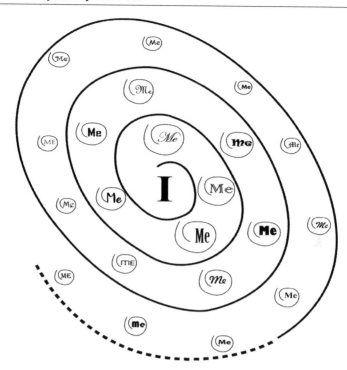

Like a gyrocompass, the self is a continuously active system that dependably points toward the "true north" of a person's perceived existence. This guidance system not only shapes the ways people view themselves, others, and the world, but it also allows a person to take a certain stance in life. This stance can be positive or negative, influenced by what happens in the school.

The ingredients of self-concept are primarily social, obtained through countless interactions with persons, places, policies, programs, and processes. As a way of interpreting oneself, individuals attribute meaning to the acts of others. For example, one child announced at the dinner table that she was an honest person. When asked how she knew she was honest, she replied, "Because my teacher asked me to help her grade papers!" Children learn

At some level of awareness each person continually asks a very basic question: "Who do you say I am?" The answer to this question influences how people behave and what they become.

to see themselves as honest just as they learn to view themselves as dishonest. The self-concepts of students are heavily influenced by those who treat them as able, valuable, and responsible, as well as those who treat them as unable, worthless, and irresponsible. At some level of awareness each person continually asks a very basic question: "Who do you say I am?" The answer to this question influences how people behave and what they become. In a sense, a person's self-concept is informed by the messages sent by others. How this information is interpreted influences how one sees oneself.

Beginning early in life infants receive countless cues as to their value in the eyes of significant others. Adults communicate these cues to the infant through their postures, facial expressions, gestures, eye contact, and other body movements as well as through their vocalizations.

Words are always accompanied by gestures that elucidate, emphasize, enhance, or even contradict the spoken word. The father who says to his small child "Of course I love you" while his eyes never leave the television set, or the teacher who speaks of her high regard for students, but shivers inside at their touch, contradict their words with their behavior. What people do "speaks" much louder than what they say. This is particularly true in schools, where inviting or disinviting messages can be recognized in every aspect of school life. This includes the people, places, policies, programs, and processes that make up a school.

Next to the home, schools probably exert the single greatest influence on how children see themselves and their abilities. The concepts that the teacher has of the students can become the concepts the students come to have of themselves.

The child is constantly construing the environment; the child affects the environment as well as being affected by it. There is a continuous and constant interaction between the child and the school. In addition to teachers' perceptions, students are also significantly influenced by how they are treated by their peers. The influences of a supportive or destructive peer group can make an important difference in all a student does.

Most elementary and secondary school students spend more than a thousand hours per year in school. Their experiences in school play a major role in determining what they think of themselves and their abilities. One student described a school experience this way:

When I was in the 5th grade, we had a variety show every Friday afternoon. One Friday I sang a song. My teacher loved the song because her husband was in the military and far away. The song was about "Sending myself to my loved one in a letter." I have always tried to please my teachers, but never have I pleased anyone so much! She embraced me, both physically and psychologically, and invited me to sing before the PTA. I've been singing ever since!

Of all the contemporary models of teaching, none depends more on the teacher's personal and professional qualities than does Invitational Education. Classroom teachers are stimulus objects, attractive or repellent in their own right. By their very presence, they have a subtle but profound impact on students' self-concepts. The teacher's task, therefore, is to behave in ways that encourage positive perceptions in students' regard of themselves and of their abilities.

From the moment students first make contact with school, the inviting or disinviting actions of school personnel—coupled with the physical environments, the official policies, the instructional programs, and the political processes—dominate their education. Students able to meet the academic expectations of schools are likely to develop positive attitudes toward themselves as learners, whereas those who fail are likely to develop negative feelings. Clearly, school profoundly influences students' development.

Self-Concept as Guidance System

Self-concept is a complex, continuously active system of subjective beliefs about personal existence. It guides behavior and enables each individual to assume particular roles in life. Rather than initiating activity, self-concept serves as a perceptual filter and guides the direction of behavior. A student's self-concept does not cause the student to misbehave in the classroom. A better explanation is that the disruptive student has learned to see himself or herself as a troublemaker and behaves accordingly. In other words, self-concept serves as the reference point, or anchoring perception, for behavior. Shavelson and Marsh (1986) refer to self-concept as a "moderator variable." In practical classroom situations, students who have learned to see themselves as troublemakers are likely to exhibit troublemaker behavior.

The student may feel that it is better to drop out of the game and be safe than to continue to play and continue to get hurt. It takes courage to continue, and good teachers work at modeling and inviting this courage.

Early on, Zimmerman and Allebrand (1965) provided research evidence regarding the guidance function of self-concept. They demonstrated that poor readers lack a sense of personal worth and adequacy to the point where they actively avoid achievement. For poor readers, to study hard and still fail provides unbearable proof of their inadequacy. To avoid such proof and thus suffer less pain, many students deliberately choose not to try. Their defense against failure is secretly to accept themselves as failures! It is better, from such a student's viewpoint, not to try than to try and be embarrassed or humiliated. A person with a negative self-concept defends the self against further loss. The student may feel that it is better to drop out of the game and be safe than to continue to play and continue to get hurt. It takes courage to continue, and good teachers work at modeling and inviting this courage.

The determining role of students' beliefs about their self-efficacy has been documented by Schunk (1989, 1990), Zimmerman et al. (1992), and others. According to self-efficacy researchers, students' positive beliefs in their efficacy in self-regulated learning affected their perceived self-efficacy in school achievement, their academic goal setting, and their subsequent academic achievement. This analysis suggests that schools should offer experiences that are intentionally designed to strengthen students' self-efficacy beliefs.

Each person acts in accordance with the ways they have learned to see themselves. From a lifetime of studying their own actions and those of significant others, individuals acquire expectations about what things "fit" in their personal worlds. For example, if a new experience is consistent with past experiences already incorporated into the self-concept system, the person easily accepts and assimilates the new experience. If the new experience contradicts those already incorporated, however, the person will probably reject it. Each person incorporates that which is congenial to the self-system already established. Furthermore, actions that are incompatible with the self-image are likely to result in psychological discomfort and anxiety. The result is that everything a person experiences is filtered through, and mediated by, whatever self-concept is already present within the individual. This screening process ensures some consistency within the human personality.

The tendency toward internal consistency appears to be a necessary feature of human personality. It provides the individual's entire being with internal balance, a sense of direction, and a feeling of stability. If individuals adopted new beliefs about themselves rapidly, or if their behaviors were capricious, no integrity would exist in the individual personality and human progress would be difficult to imagine. Few people would risk flying if they thought the pilots might suddenly perceive themselves as Captain Marvel! Fortunately, most people are remarkably consistent in their self-concepts.

Being correct in one's assumptions about oneself has reward value, even if the assumption is negative.

Educators who are not aware of the conservative nature of self-concept are likely to expect quick or miraculous changes in others—such as the teacher who commented, "I'm not going to send another student to the counseling office. I sent a student yesterday. Today he's back and he hasn't changed a bit!" Self-perceptions do change, but not immediately or automatically.

One probable reason for the apparent failure of many school programs designed to enhance, build, or modify students' perceptions of themselves is the tendency to overlook the conservative nature of self-concept. Whether a student's self-perception is psychologically healthy or unhealthy, educationally productive or counterproductive, the student will cling to it the way a drowning person clings to a straw. In fact, students who have learned to see themselves as stupid will experience considerable anxiety over their own successful performance. Students who have learned to expect failure are even likely to sabotage their own efforts when they meet unexpected success. They actively maintain their self-pictures even if the pictures are false and unhealthy.

One additional point relates to the consistency of self-concept: Being correct in one's assumptions about oneself has reward value, even if the assumption is negative. A student may take a certain pleasure in thinking, "See, just as I thought, I knew nobody in this lousy school cares whether I live or die!" Being right, even about negative feelings toward oneself, can be satisfying. This is one reason why one-shot attempts, quick-fix efforts, or programs that lack consistency in philosophy and dependability in direction are often unsuccessful and may even incur student resistance or anger.

Although self-concepts tend toward consistency, changes in self-concepts are possible. New ideas filter into the self-concept throughout life, while some old ideas fade away. This continuous process creates flexibility in human personality and allows psychological development. The hypothetical reason for the assimilation of new ideas and the expulsion of old ones is that each person has a basic need to maintain, protect, and enhance the self-concept—to obtain positive self-regard as well as positive regard from others. This basic human characteristic is a tremendous given for the classroom teacher.

Significance of Positive Self-Regard

A person who doubts himself [sic] is like a man who would enlist in the ranks of his enemies and bear arms against himself. He makes his failure certain by himself being the first person to be convinced of it.

—Alexandre Dumas, *The Three Musketeers*, 1844

To learn in school, students require sufficient confidence in themselves and their abilities to make some effort to succeed. Self-regard and efforts to control one's destiny correlate highly. The more self-esteem a person has, the greater, as a rule, is his desire and his ability to control himself. Without self-confidence, students easily succumb to apathy, dependency, and loss of self-control. Too often, the real problem of negative self-esteem is hidden beneath such labels as *unmotivated, unteachable, undisciplined, unable,* or *uninterested.* The classroom result is that students with low self-regard will expect the worst in every situation and will be constantly afraid of saying the wrong word or doing the wrong thing.

The importance of self-efficacy and self-regard has been documented by Coopersmith's classic study of the antecedents of self-esteem among children. Coopersmith (1967) reported: "There are pervasive and significant differences in the experiential worlds and social behaviors of persons who differ in self-esteem. Persons high in their own self-estimation approach tasks as persons with the expectation that they will be well-received and successful" (p. 70). Similar findings of other researchers (Chapman, 1988; Covington, 1984; Hattie, 1992; Tesser & Campbell, 1983) show that individuals high in self-esteem are more independent of external reinforcement and more consistent in their social behavior.

Research also provides evidence that people with negative self-regard tend to be more destructive, more anxious, more stressed, and more likely to manifest psychosomatic symptoms than people of average or high self-regard. Although feeling worthless is not the same as being worthless, the impact on student behavior is often the same. "I never raise my hand in class," a high school student wrote. "I guess it goes back to elementary school; when I asked my teacher about a question [problem], she responded, 'Oh, that's the easiest problem in the chapter; anyone can figure that out.'" Whether intentional or unintentional, a disinviting comment can have lasting and devastating effects on self-esteem.

From an invitational perspective, one of the most damaging things a teacher can teach a child is not to try. Even if something does not work, the student has learned something. Perhaps the only real failure in life is to fail to try.

What research findings and student reports on the importance of self-regard mean for educators is that many common classroom problems, such as student disruption, inattention, apathy, and anxiety, probably indicate negative self-regard in the students exhibiting such behavior.

Research on classroom discipline reveals a significant relationship between students' low self-concepts as learners and their misbehavior in the classroom. Branch et al. (1977) evaluated disruptive and nondisruptive middle-school students (grades 5 through 8) on their professed and inferred academic self-concepts. Analysis revealed significant differences between the two groups. Those students identified by their behavior as disruptive had significantly lower self-concepts as learners than did students identified as nondisruptive. The study's theoretical implication was that the students' negative feelings about themselves as learners might be a contributing factor in student disruption. Related research in the relationship between self-concept and social functioning in adolescence (Ybrandt, 2008) indicates that adolescents 15–16 years of age had a stronger relationship between a negative self-concept and externalizing problem behavior than younger or older youth. Self-concept may eventually prove to be a significant mediating variable that will help educators understand many types of seemingly unrelated behavior problems.

Compounding the problem of negative self-regard is the apparent correlation between a person's self-regard and the degree to which they are disturbed by the poor opinion of others. Students are highly sensitive to the behavior of others toward them, and their feelings can remain injured for many years, creating a downward spiraling effect on self-regard. One teacher revealed the long-term impact of real or imagined slights thusly:

> Several years ago, a young man, now the assistant manager of a large grocery store, stopped me at the counter and said: "You don't remember me, do you?" I replied that I remembered his face and that he had been a student of mine. Since at least ten years had passed, I could not remember his name. His remark that followed stunned me. I did not try to argue or insist that I had never said it. Instead I said: "I only hope that I never said such a thing to you or to any other student. I hope you are doing well." I walked away, wondering if I were guilty, if I had—in disgust, anger, or frustration—said it. I made a commitment never to let it happen again. This is what the assistant manager told me I said to him: "Right before I quit school, you told me that I'd never amount to anything. You see. I've proved you wrong."

Behavior is guided by self-concept; whether real or imagined, a teacher's disinviting message has the potential to take on its own life and exist for many years, particularly in the minds of students already unsure of their own worth and ability. As House (1992) demonstrated, academic self-concept is continuously modified on the basis of perceived school experiences.

SUMMARY

This chapter explored the three essential foundations of Invitational Education: The democratic ethos, perceptual tradition, and self-concept theory. Democratic ethos was shown to be the guiding ideal that points to ever-enriching communicative processes—processes that promote the development of all in a pluralistic society. The perceptual tradition was described as a focus on the individual's world of experience, the learning of personal reality, and the ability to reflect upon the perceptions and imagine various creative possibilities for the future. Self-concept theory was presented to show how a person's perceived self develops primarily from inviting or disinviting messages sent, received, interpreted, and acted upon. There is a strong tendency to protect one's self-concept against conflicting pressures, to think as well of oneself as social and emotional circumstances permit, and to want to be regarded positively by significant others. Educators have a better chance of successfully dealing with complex situations in an inviting way if they work to internalize the inner and ethical logic of these three foundations.

Chapter 3 examines the stance necessary to maintain an intentionally inviting perspective and sets the stage for the development of practical skills and the handling of challenging situations presented in Chapters 4 and 5.

Further Reflections and Activities

1. *Democratic Ethos:* School secretaries, custodians, security guards, and teacher assistants often report feeling like "second-class citizens" when not included in discussions about procedural changes or provided with important information in a timely fashion. How can school leaders give voice to these important stakeholders and demonstrate that they value the school's support staff?

2. *Perceptual Tradition:* Think of a situation when you were very upset about a student's inappropriate behavior. Rewind to the moment when you approached the student, perhaps not fully aware of what might have triggered the behavior. How might you begin a nonjudgmental conversation with the student to gather more information and better understand his or her perspective before determining what should happen next?

3. *Self-Concept Theory:* Select a student or colleague that you interact with often, who often demonstrates a negative attitude or choice of behavior. During the next few weeks, try to find opportunities to acknowledge some talent, strength, or characteristic about the person that you admire or appreciate. Observe how the person responds to you. What changes do you notice in their behavior or your relationship with that person?

The Inviting Mindset

I have never met a star teacher clutching a grade book, or averaging grades based on test scores, or taking papers home simply to grade them, or meeting with parents just to share grades, or using grades as the primary basis for recommending retention, or grouping children on the bases of grades, or happily entering grades on permanent records, or using grades to explain to a child how well he or she is progressing. (Haberman, 1995, p. 13)

In the abstract, Invitational Education can sound too good to be true. It is a positive approach to working with people, and most educators can see a value to this mindset. In the often harsh realities of everyday practice, however, it takes persistence, resourcefulness, and courage to make the intentionally inviting stance a self-correcting way to work with oneself and others.

To be consistently inviting with oneself and others, personally and professionally, educators require an understanding of the democratic ethos, the perceptual tradition, and self-concept theory, as introduced in Chapter 2. The goal is to apply this understanding in actual situations involving real people. This understanding involves the artful blending of perceptions, stance, and behaviors into a working theory of practice.

Invitational Theory (the theoretical construct of Invitational Education) serves as a framework for guidance and reflection as educators put Invitational Education into practice in everyday communication, actions, and decisions. Without such a framework for reference, individuals and school systems struggle to improve interpersonal communication as well as the overall climate of the school. The Illustration of Invitational Theory provided in Figure 3.1 provides a "big picture" reference as we continue to introduce the components of Invitational Education. The components in each column appear in the order that they are presented in this book, starting at the bottom and working upward. Each component builds upon the one that comes before, helping us develop in skill and understanding over time.

Figure 3.1: An Illustration of Invitational Theory

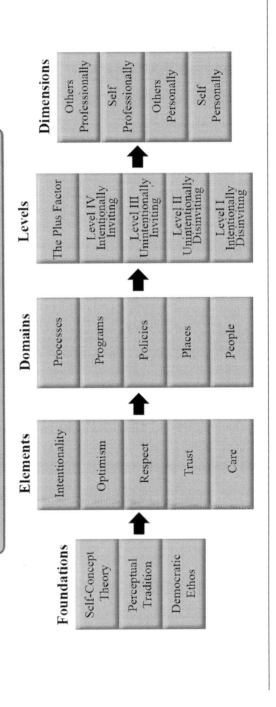

PERCEPTIONS OF PROFESSIONAL HELPERS

Teachers who have been in classrooms for any length of time know that teaching is a fragile, sometimes puzzling process. Things can go well when least expected, whereas the best-prepared lesson can fail. Teachers play an important role in the success of the classroom. As explained in Chapter 2, people behave according to the particular beliefs they hold about themselves, others, and the world. Teachers who believe that students are able, valuable, and responsible are well on their way to becoming the sort of teacher and leader advocated in this book.

No single explanation can cover the complexity of the educative process. It is increasingly evident, however, that the teacher's perceptions of students, as reflected in teacher behavior, have the power to influence how students view themselves and how well they learn in school.

Like a sculptor who envisions something in a block of marble that others cannot see, the inviting teacher perceives possibilities in students that others miss. Effective helpers in many professions—including teaching, counseling, nursing, the ministry, and public service—can be distinguished from less effective helpers on the basis of their perceptions. This finding was first introduced in the classic *Florida Studies in the Helping Professions* (Combs et al., 1969.) There is a high degree of similarity among the belief systems of "good helpers" in numerous professional fields. Good teachers, for example, may be clearly distinguished from poor ones on the basis of their perceptions of people as able rather than unable, friendly rather than unfriendly, worthy rather than unworthy, dependable rather than undependable, helpful rather than hindering, and internally rather than externally focused.

> *Like a sculptor who envisions something in a block of marble that others cannot see, the inviting teacher perceives possibilities in students that others miss.*

Growing evidence supports two important assumptions of Invitational Education. First, inviting and disinviting messages primarily result from perceptions. Second, these messages significantly affect students' self-concepts as well as their attitudes toward school, the relationships they form in school, and their school achievement. Children feel more connected to school and are committed to academic learning when they are surrounded by a caring and supportive school environment.

Clearly, educators should work on developing their positive perceptions of themselves, others, and education if they wish to be a beneficial presence in students' lives. Positive perception means viewing students as able, valuable, and responsible, as well as seeing oneself and education in essentially favorable ways. These teacher perceptions are worth considering in greater detail.

Viewing Students as Able

As presented in Chapter 1, an important assumption of Invitational Education is that each student has relatively untapped capabilities for thinking, choosing, and learning and that these capabilities can be realized in an optimally inviting school environment. This assumption is supported by what is known about the capabilities of children.

From birth, infants are marvelously curious, seeming to obtain a sense of pleasure and satisfaction from understanding and mastering their environments. From a very young age, children rapidly acquire knowledge, which they apply to gain further understanding of their environments.

Today educators recognize that children possess far greater capacities for learning than almost anyone previously had thought possible. Human intelligence is currently recognized as a dynamic potential, rather than a static entity. This mental functioning level can be strongly influenced by either facilitating or debilitating environments. Most students develop a desire for further learning when they are provided with a favorable social and emotional climate.

Throughout their school years, some students become more creative, some less so; some become excited about learning, some become bored and disillusioned; some become intellectually active, some less active. Some students fall in love with books, others learn to hate them. Some develop a passion for physical exercise, others learn to avoid it. The entire process is heavily influenced by the belief systems of teachers as manifested in their actions.

In addition to their actual classroom presence, students exist as mental images in teachers' minds. Teachers who believe that certain children cannot learn or benefit from instruction will have little success in teaching them. If educators believe that half the people cannot think for themselves, they will establish a school system that will actually make it impossible for half of the people to think for themselves.

Happily, when teachers have positive views of students' abilities, students are likely to respond in positive ways. This process was documented by a student who wrote, "I am 21 and a painting major. When I was in the sixth grade I suggested a mural design for our school. My teacher was so pleased she ordered the paint, ladder, even excused me from regular class so I could complete the mural. I usually tire of my past work, or don't think it's very good, yet I still believe that mural was one of the best paintings I've ever done. I think it turned out so well because the teacher had such faith in my ability." Students develop best when they share the company of teachers who see them as possessing relatively untapped abilities in myriad areas and who invite them to realize their potential.

A beautiful example of how perceptions determine behavior was provided by Scott Robinson in a personal communication with the authors.

Scott is a professor at the University of Hawaii at Manoa. Scott describes this encounter with a young student teacher who believed that students are valuable.

> Recently, I visited a middle school math class to observe one of my student teachers. As I entered the classroom, I noticed that students were quietly working on math problems at their desks as the student teacher circulated among them. I was in a hurry so I walked quickly towards the student teacher. Just as I started to speak, a nearby student raised her hand and looked up from her paper. The student teacher promptly turned her back to me, stopped at the student's desk, and began engaging the student on the math problem. I stopped in my tracks at first disappointed that the student teacher ignored me. I felt disappointed and insulted.
>
> Then, after a moment, it dawned on me that the student teacher was being invitational with the middle school student. The student teacher taught me a lesson in being humble and invitational. Humble in that I am not the center of the learning community in the student teacher's classroom. Invitational since the student teacher conveyed respect, optimism, and care with her students. I respected the student teacher for putting the needs of her middle school students first. Her student-centeredness reminded me that my own needs as a university supervisor are secondary when it comes to student teachers being invitational with their students in the middle school classroom.

Many schools are making significant progress in viewing and treating children with special needs in more positive ways. Instead of referring to children as "special education students," or "learning disabled," a preferred term—"exceptional children"—is being encouraged. Exceptional children refers to children whose performance is superior and who require more challenging instruction, as well as those with learning difficulties or physical or behavioral problems that require modification of the educational regimen in order to help them learn (Heward, 2012).

Our exceptional children are being welcomed into the mainstream as valued members of inclusion classes. Rather than looking at inclusion as a special education initiative, inclusion classes become ways to embrace our diversity. "We all have strengths, we all have stretches, and we all need to get better at something. The difference in teaching to diversity, however, is that we don't start with our deficits; we start with our strengths" (Moore 2017, p. iii).

A successful inclusion class relies on caring relationships between the co-teachers and all students in the class. Here are just a few considerations to keep in mind while managing the complexities of multiple instructors and diverse learners in one classroom:

- Teachers feel equally valued when they share the leadership of the classroom, so that the special education teacher is not treated like an assistant to the general education teacher. Time is provided for them to collaborate, review student progress, and share strategies that benefit all students in the class.
- Behavioral issues may be triggered when a student struggles with learning and feels humiliated or embarrassed. Digital resources that permit students to review grades, self-assess, and indicate a need for assistance privately to the teachers on a device are helpful, and respect students' privacy. A reading assignment can be offered digitally in different versions to match different levels of reading comprehension so that all students can participate in a discussion on the same topic.
- Teachers strive to look at *their* choice of language, policies, and processes in the classroom through an inviting lens. Are some students not following directions because they are not paying attention, or is the teacher giving too many directions at one time for them to process? When a student disrupts the class is the teacher's first response to issue a consequence or to be curious and identify student feelings and needs?
- It is preferable to work with all students in mixed groups, with both the general education and special education teacher working with all students. This provides valuable opportunities for students to help each other and develop relationships.
- When at all possible, students do not leave the classroom for other services that might be needed. Interventions occur within the regular classroom.

In a successful inclusion class, students are unaware of who has an Individual Education Plan, and all students benefit from the diverse learning strategies used and gain a sense of belonging.

Perceiving Students as Valuable

When professional helpers believe that each student or client is a person of value, their behavior will reflect this belief. People constantly communicate their real feelings in the "silent language"—the language of behavior. When teachers perceive their students positively, they are more likely to involve themselves with their students both personally and professionally, and a doing-with as opposed to a doing-to process often results. The warmth of this teacher-student partnership is illustrated by a middle school student who wrote, "Mr. Russell is my best teacher, and he asked me to remind him to watch his weight—and I do, too!"

Education is, or should be, a cooperative enterprise. An atmosphere of mutual respect and positive regard increases the likelihood of cooperation and student success in school. This positive social and emotional atmosphere is particularly important in working with students who are alienated, isolated, or who demonstrate challenging behaviors. Today's educators are doing a much better job of addressing the needs of students by not labeling a student as "disadvantaged" or "at-risk." Instead of referring to a student as an "at-risk student," or a "challenging student," we are making efforts to refer to them simply as students who exhibit "challenging behaviors." In this way we are focusing on what is causing the child's choice of behavior, rather than judging the child.

With the help of our mental health professionals, educators are learning more about Adverse Childhood Experiences (ACEs) and applying this knowledge to how they see and help their students. In a helpful guide, *Preventing Adverse Childhood Experience,* (2019), the Centers for Disease Control and Prevention provides the following description of ACEs:

> Adverse Childhood Experiences, or ACEs, are potentially traumatic events that occur in childhood (0-17 years) such as experiencing violence, abuse, or neglect; witnessing violence in the home; and having a family member attempt or die by suicide. Also included are aspects of the child's environment that can undermine their sense of safety, stability, and bonding such as growing up in a household with substance misuse, mental health problems, or instability due to parental separation or incarceration of a parent, sibling or other member of the household.
>
> Traumatic events in childhood can be emotionally painful or distressing and can have effects that persist for years. Factors such as the nature, frequency and seriousness of the traumatic event, prior history of trauma, and available family and community supports can shape a child's response to trauma. . . . ACEs and associated conditions such as living in under-resourced or racially segregated neighborhoods, frequently moving, experiencing food insecurity, and other instability can cause toxic stress. (pp. 7–8)

The report also sheds light on advances in brain research which identify biological changes that may contribute to behaviors that cause children to struggle in school:

> A large and growing body of research indicates that toxic stress during childhood can harm the most basic levels of the nervous, endocrine, and immune systems, and that such exposures can even alter the physical structure of DNA (epigenetic effects). Changes to the brain from toxic stress can affect such things as attention, impulsive behavior, decision-making, learning, emotion, and response to stress. (p. 8)

When school leaders are aware of and share such findings with staff, the school takes a giant leap forward in seeing all students as able, valuable, and responsible. Instead of blaming children or giving up on them, educators strive to be a consistently dependable, and positive person in each child's life.

Toxic stress can be found in homes in all sectors of society but is exacerbated by a lack of resources. Many of the challenges that teachers face can be traced to homes where adult caregivers are themselves under great pressures and constraints to provide food, shelter, clothing, safety, jobs, and stability. Ruby Payne (2018) has pointed out how children of poverty are in deep need of caring relationships, especially in cases where they do not have a belief of a positive future. For Payne, children who come to school psychologically, intellectually, socially, and/or emotionally undernourished are in deep need of teachers, leaders, and schools that intentionally and actively appreciate their value.

Teachers who view students as valuable and communicate this to their students often have tremendous success in helping a disengaged student change their approach to school. For example, Shyheim, a high school student in Mrs. Worth's drawing class:

Shyheim showed interest and talent in drawing. Yet, he was often late to school and failing most of his classes. One day he informed Mrs. Worth that he wouldn't be around much after basketball season ended. He had been making it to just enough classes each day to be eligible for afterschool practices.

Mrs. Worth talked with Shyheim about his engaging personality and talent for drawing. She told him that there were many things that he did well, and she wanted him to use his talents. In fact, she planned to make a life size oil painting of Shyheim from a photograph she took of him. Shyheim watched each day as the painting came to life. Mrs. Worth told him that if he came to all of his classes and did not miss a day of school through the end of the year, she would give him the oil painting.

Shyheim started coming to school regularly, making wonderful sketches in Mrs. Worth's class and surprisingly catching up in all of his academic classes. On the day that Mrs. Worth presented the oil painting to Shyheim, one of the authors came to meet him. Shyheim was beaming. He explained how he liked teaching the kids in the neighborhood how to play basketball. He shared that he thought he was a good listener and wanted to be a psychologist. That summer, the school was able to secure a counseling job for Shyheim, working with young children. Somehow his mother managed to get him a ride to the camp. Shyheim became a favorite counselor and never missed a day.

As Levitt and Dubner (2014) point out, poverty is a symptom of the absence of a workable democratic process built on credible political, social, and legal institutions. Having said this, the failure of society does not excuse educators from putting their hearts into their work, using their knowledge, experience, and imaginations to invite chil-dren to realize their immeasurable potential in all areas of worthwhile endeavor. Although educators cannot do everything, they can do something. This something can be wonderfully life-changing for a child.

> *When teachers believe in each student's value, they telegraph this belief in everything they do and in every way they do it.*

   These and other findings indicate that it is vital that educators develop and maintain a positive view of all students. One additional reason for seeing students as valuable is that such a view may contribute significantly to their men-tal health. Feelings of worthlessness characterize a suffering personality. Teachers signal their positive beliefs in countless ways. One student wrote,

> My third-grade teacher . . . I was new in the school (in the middle of the year) and was lonely, shy, alone. It was a cold, winter day and I had a cold. I sneezed very hard and didn't have a tissue. I tried to hide it in my hand, in a fist. Mrs. Benedict very tactfully brought me a tissue and slipped it in my hand. I was very thankful.

When teachers believe in each student's value, they telegraph this belief in everything they do and in every way they do it.

Seeing Students as Responsible

In schools today, the number of things a student can be ordered or coerced to do is, or should be, kept to a minimum. Both student desire and per-formance tend to deteriorate when external controls such as threats, sur-veillance, punishment, and bribes are used. Deci's and Ryan's research on self-determination theory found that controls—whether they be rewards or consequences—consume part of our limited working attention needed to do a task, leaving less of our attention to focus on the task (Deci, 1995, p. 51).

   As we defined it in Chapter 1, motivation is a given for each person. Without it a person would not be able to do anything. Since motivation, the impetus to maintain, protect, and enhance one's self-concept, lies within each of us, educators should not be expected to—and, actually, cannot—motivate others. Rather, the educator's job is to *create the conditions* that will help students to become motivated to make responsible decisions. These conditions include:

- *autonomy*—a sense of choice, whether it be the topic, the way a project might be completed, or whom one can work with;
- *competence*—the ability to complete a task successfully, which messages us that effort is worth it and encourages us to accept higher challenges; and
- *relatedness*—a positive connection to the teacher, the others in the class, or the topic. (Deci, 1995)

From an inviting perspective, a teacher cannot "learn" a student. Students choose to learn, just as they choose not to learn, to give up, in the face of ridicule, embarrassment, or coercion. Invitational Education builds on the assumption that students will elect to learn those things they perceive to be significant in their personal lives. The teacher's task is to create social, emotional, and intellectual conditions in which students will direct their motivation in positive ways for themselves and others.

Choice for teachers is equally important. In these times of control-oriented approaches to school reform like high-stakes testing, score-based teacher evaluation, and overly standardized curricula, teachers are experiencing diminishing choices in what and how they can teach. It takes a skillful and inviting school leader to recognize this negative consequence and find ways to ensure teachers still experience a sense of choice and competence in their work. Telling teachers or students to do something because it is on the test is an educationally defeating mantra that is being heard more and more. One of the authors talked with a stressed student in a high school classroom who was agonizingly memorizing a long list of words for a chemistry test. When asked if he understood the words the student said emphatically, "No!" When asked if he wanted to understand the concepts underlying the words, the student even more emphatically said, "No! I tried understanding the concepts but it got in the way of doing well on the test."

Teachers who recognize the definite limits of their powers to make students learn are in a good position to try alternative ways of teaching. These teachers can more easily find their own best ways of inviting students to discover the personal pleasure of self-directed learning. For example, a Minnesota high school science teacher was so successful at inviting students to learn science that some students continued to attend his class even after dropping out of school! One such "drop-in" en route to this science class was intercepted by a secretary, who demanded to know why this drop-out was in the building. The science teacher, overhearing the question, quietly took the secretary aside and said, "Our job is not to ask students why they're here; our job is to ask them why they're not here." Several days later, the principal asked another of the teacher's drop-ins why he continued to attend class. The boy responded, "Frankly, I just want to see what he's gonna do next!"

By respecting students and believing in their ability, value, and self-directing powers, teachers can spend less time trying to force students to learn and more energy developing an exciting and appealing environment in which learning can occur. While attending a conference, one of the authors had the good fortune to enjoy a meal with two esteemed colleagues, Leo Buscaglia and Harry Wong. During the dinner, Leo described a beautiful analogy of how this might be accomplished. He used the metaphor of knowledge being a marvelous feast. What the teacher can do is prepare food with great relish and care, sample it frequently, dance around the table at mealtime, and invite students to join the celebration! This approach seems to make better sense than trying to force-feed unwilling students—and is certainly more gratifying. Choice and feelings of personal responsibility promote school achievement. The apparent rule is that when students are given meaningful choices in their education, they are likely to follow through on assignments, as well as learn and remember more, for they are learning what they have elected to learn.

Finally, a belief in people's ability to make intelligent choices is the foundation of a democratic way of life. When Thomas Jefferson wrote the Declaration of Independence, he never wavered in his faith that people, when free to choose, will find their own best ways. He believed that if individuals were unable to handle freedom of choice, the remedy was not to take it away from them but to inform them by education. Similarly, John Dewey proclaimed throughout his career that the best cure for the problems of democracy is more democracy. When students are encouraged to make significant choices in their lives, they are far more likely, later in life, to maintain personal integrity in the face of external pressure and manipulation. They are also more likely to support a democratic philosophy of government.

Educators can better facilitate student responsibility when they hold certain perceptions about themselves. Self-confidence, self-efficacy, and positive self-regard are associated with success as a professional helper.

Viewing Oneself Positively

Perceiving students as able, valuable, and responsible is much easier when educators have a positive and realistic view of themselves. A growing body of literature in the education, psychology, and counseling fields centers on the assumption that when teachers better understand, accept, and like themselves, they have a much greater capacity to understand, accept, and like students. A positive, realistic view of oneself is an important ingredient in behaving in an inviting manner. "Mrs. Reynolds expected good things of us," a high school student wrote, "and we could tell she also expected good things of herself."

The ability to speak to oneself about oneself in positive, realistic ways is an important aspect of Invitational Education. Positive self-talk has been associated with the effectiveness of professional helpers (Fugua et al., 1986; Purkey 2000; Stanley, 1991). To understand this, imagine two science teachers. Both possess essentially the same knowledge and skills. During each teacher's class, two students carry on a private conversation, ignoring the carefully prepared demonstration by the teacher. This student behavior elicits different internal dialogues (what we say to ourselves about ourselves, sometimes called self-talk) from the two teachers. The first teacher thinks, "I've stayed up half the night to prepare this demonstration, and those two students are not paying a bit of attention to me. I know I'm not the greatest teacher, but why do kids have to be so rude?" The second teacher, faced with exactly the same student behavior, is more positive and realistic and thinks something like this: "Those two students are not paying attention. That's too bad because this is an important and well-prepared demonstration. I will rethink the dynamics of this demonstration. Meanwhile, after class I'll talk to these students about the reasons for their lack of attention."

Educators who are personally and professionally inviting not only have positive perceptions about themselves and others; they also have rich and extensive perceptions about the subjects they desire to teach.

The first teacher's perceptions and internal dialogue are self-defeating. They exaggerate the meaning of the students' behavior, they emphasize the two students' lack of attention over the attention of all the other students in the class, and they overgeneralize the situation by assuming personal inadequacy. Clearly, the first teacher's internal dialogue is inappropriate, anxiety producing, and self-defeating. The second teacher makes a more positive appraisal of the classroom situation and forms a more realistic and constructive pattern of internal selfstatements.

Awareness of one's internal dialogue and realistic appraisals of classroom experiences play an important role in teachers' adaptive or maladaptive behavior. Teachers are too often overly critical in what they say to themselves about themselves. "The worst enemies of teachers," as one teacher noted, "are teachers!" An important way to become more personally and professionally inviting is to be gentle with oneself, to be aware of self-defeating perceptions, and to practice positive and productive self-statements.

Perceiving oneself positively also means applying the categories able, valuable, and responsible to one's own existence. The perception that people are worthy of inviting, that they have relatively untapped potential, and that they can make meaningful choices in their lives applies to oneself as well as to others. Positive and realistic perceptions of the self are essential parts of the inviting approach to education. The same is true regarding positive perceptions of education.

Perceiving Education Affirmatively

Teaching is a delicate relationship between and among people aiming at a positive, enduring attitude to learning. Teaching involves knowing something worth knowing and desiring to share and extend this knowledge with others. Educators who are personally and professionally inviting not only have positive perceptions about themselves and others; they also have rich and extensive perceptions about the subjects they desire to teach. One student said, "Because Mr. Chambers opened up so many doors of knowledge to us, I felt smarter and eager to learn."

An example of a powerful summons to learning is found in *The Once and Future King*, where Merlin is talking to Wart (the future King Arthur):

> "The best thing for being sad," replied Merlyn, beginning to puff and blow, "is to learn something. That is the only thing that never fails. You may grow old and trembling in your anatomies, you may lie awake at night listening to the disorder of your veins, you may miss your only love, you may see the world about you devastated by evil lunatics, or know your honor trampled in the sewers of baser minds. There is only one thing for it then to learn. Learn why the world wags and what wags it. That is the only thing which the mind can never exhaust, never alienate, never be tortured by, never fear or distrust, and never dream of regretting. Learning is the thing for you." (White, 1958, pp. 185–186)

Involved in the process of extending invitations to learning is the teacher's personal relationship to the content and essence of what they teach. A teacher who can perceive meaning, clarity, significance, and excitement in what they teach is better able to invite students to do likewise. In addition, the likelihood of an invitation to learning being accepted increases when the teacher is perceived as having expertise, enthusiasm, and sound judgment, as well as being seen as caring and trustworthy. These events are most likely to emerge when the teacher develops and maintains a social and emotional stance that promotes positive relationships and serves as a basis for subsequent action.

TEACHER STANCE

Invitational Education is a theory of practice; that is, it is about putting perceptions to work. To exist, invitations must be sent and received; they cannot merely be wished for. People do not reach their potential because others simply wish them well. Thus, Invitational Education practitioners exhibit a consistent behavioral framework. The term "teacher stance" is useful here to indicate the general position from which one operates and one's typical pattern of action.

In baseball, a stance is the unique way a batter digs in to make solid contact with the ball. Although no one stance is perfect, there are some basic mechanics. Players must develop a stance that is sound, comfortable, and deserving of their confidence in order to focus their attention on efforts to make the right connection. Likewise, a teacher's stance involves uniqueness, personal ownership, and functional criteria. The stance focuses a teacher's perceptions so the teacher can make solid contact. Although it cannot guarantee success, a good stance makes it more likely that beneficial things will happen. Stance goes beyond beliefs in that it is action-oriented and gives life to goals, purposes, and attitudes.

In Invitational Education, a teacher's good stance is built around five elements: care, trust, respect, optimism, and intentionality. These elements serve as an operating system from which we can all make more beneficial choices of words and action. To make sustainable change in schools, *all* school adults should be invited to learn about and practice invitational strategies. Our experiences with schools tell us that staff members will respond very positively to these strategies, especially when a school's leader is also willing to be reflective about his or her own communication skills. Leaders who have employed a "doing to" approach will likely need to share with the staff that they are committed to using Invitational Education to improve their skills. The school's leadership team, no matter how control-oriented or judgmental their messages may have been in the past, will be able to gain trust and buy-in from staff, as long as they are genuinely willing to learn and practice along with everyone else.

Care

Care provides the relational core for the inviting stance. Without this core the other four elements run the risk of becoming free-floating, sweet-sounding pie in the sky. This concrete caring is the glue that directs trust, respect, optimism, and intentionality in inviting relationships. It is made manifest in the simple bonding connections educators consistently make with others. Without this sense of caring, a person is just going through the motions. To paraphrase an old song, "It don't mean a thing if you ain't got that care."

The concept of an ethics of care used in Invitational Education comes from the work of Nel Noddings (1984, 2005) and focuses on calling forth and sustaining the caring impulse, the desire to meaningfully connect with and participate in the presence and growth of another person (Novak et al., 2014). In concrete practice, this means being receptive to the perspective of another person and finding ways to use this connection to call forth their educational well-being. This caring approach is not about abstract theorizing, about consequences or duty, but a real concern with how to connect with this person now in this unique situation.

To be humane in one's caring means to expand the self to include more diverse others. This expansion of the self can move a person to feel and understand the perspectives of those initially beyond one's comfort level of familiarity. This is a powerful leap of commitment and involves developing a larger integrative framework. Humaneness requires the expansion of the self to include as many others as possible, perhaps, in the case of the saints, to include all humanity. Steven Pinker (2011) fortunately points out that this larger integrative perspective is becoming a greater part of more people's outlook, as the world is brought closer, so according to his research and analysis the better angels of our nature seem to be winning.

To be a caring invitational educator means to be able to take the focus away from oneself and attend to the interests and meanings that matter to the other person. This involves getting beyond the preoccupation that "it's all about me." Ability to extend the caring impulse to others is a key part of the dynamic of inviting oneself and others, personally and professionally. The caring impulse needs to be continually refreshed to meet the multiple challenges of today's schools.

Trust

Trust is indispensable to the inviting process. Invitational Education is most likely to thrive in an atmosphere of trust. Educators who wish to become more personally and professionally inviting develop this trusting atmosphere by believing in themselves and consistently behaving in a positive, reasonable, and dependable manner. This involves maintaining a warm, caring relationship with others, one in which educators can be "real" with themselves and others.

> *To be a caring invitational educator means to take the attention away from oneself and attend to the interests and meanings that matter to the other person.*

Invitational Education is a cooperative, collaborative activity in which process is a wedded partner to product. Support for this assumption is provided by Bergman and Gaitskill (1990), who reported that students valued teachers' trustworthy relationships with students even above professional competence.

In professions other than education, trust is viewed as a critical variable in relationships. Ouchi (1981) developed a model for successful management ("Theory Z") that emphasized the values of consensual decisionmaking. Theory Z was the forerunner of such popular innovations as "quality circles," and "site-based management." On a federal level, Etienne Wenger's (2000) work on *Communities of Practice* has inspired federal policy decisionmaking to move from a top-down to a bottom-up approach. For example, revisions to the *Individuals with Disabilities Act* are being formulated by the IDEA Partnership, which represents 50 national organizations, using a decisionmaking model called *Leading by Convening* (Cashman et al., 2014).

Within education, trust is established and maintained through sources identified by Arceneaux (1994). These sources include, but are not restricted to, *reliability* (consistency, dependability, and predictability), *genuineness* (authenticity and congruence), *truthfulness* (honesty, correctness of opinion, and validity of assertion), and *competence* (intelligent behavior, expertness, and knowledge). Educators, by being reliable, genuine, truthful, and competent, inspire trust in students and colleagues. Without trust, it is unlikely that anything of positive significance will occur in classrooms or schools.

Respect

A third important aspect of a teacher's stance deals with respect. Nothing in Invitational Education is more important than respect for people. Respect should be unconditional. Every person deserves to be treated in a respectful way, even if we disagree with their choice of action. Respectful treatment does not negate the importance of taking effective and caring action to handle unacceptable behavior.

Arnold and Roach (1989), in their study of teachers' nonverbal behaviors, reported that teachers who demonstrated respect for students through such simple processes as starting and ending class on time tended to have students who viewed the class as important and therefore tended to study more. Goffin (1989) offered a series of practical suggestions on ways that teachers can demonstrate respect for students. She suggested that teachers should develop an appreciation for each student's uniqueness. Central to this teacher perspective is appreciating cultural differences and valuing the rich complexity of each human being. This agrees with the thinking of Dewey (1930), who pointed out in *Individualism Old and New* that being a unique member of a meaningful group is important for both the individual and the group. In fact, Dewey felt that the more democratic a group is, the more the group experience builds on the unique perspectives and interests of its members, and thus the more the group experience becomes a source of educational development for all involved.

As an example, one of the authors had the pleasure of watching a unit from the United States Army present a drill. As the units performed, the observer could spot African dance, British precision drill, Native American movements, Japanese Bushido, and assorted other influences. The artful integration of many traditions was spectacular.

Respect in the school means that whatever a classroom should be, it should not be a place where people are embarrassed, insulted, humiliated, or subjected to prejudice. If there are policies, practices, or programs that cannot be performed in accordance with respect, or if there are faculty, administrators, or staff who cannot or will not function in a consistently respectful manner, they should not be in schools. Demeaning practices such as public ridicule, invidious comparisons, monocultural thinking, autocratic processes, deliberate humiliation, sexual, racial, or homophobic reactions, and corporal punishment cannot exist in a school that considers itself inviting.

Optimism

Optimists do better in school, succeed more at life tasks, and even age better and live longer (Seligman, 2006). By working to develop an optimistic perspective, educators are on the path to a good and successful life. This optimism involves both self and others and in fact is in sync with major reports about the positive direction of world development (Pinker, 2018; Rosling, 2018). A case can be made that things are getting better if we look at trendlines rather than headlines for issues like health, education, freedoms, prosperity, especially if you compare life for the average person now with, say, life in the 18th century.

Invitational Education presents a positive vision of human existence: that individuals are able, valuable, and responsible and should be treated accordingly. This starkly contrasts with the view of those who find value in pessimism and cynicism. What educator has not heard the doomsday reports of those coworkers who arrive at schools with such cynical comments as:

- "What can you expect from people like that?"
- "They don't want to learn."
- "Well, you know how they are."
- "They have no motivation."
- "They take no pride."
- "They simply don't have the ability."
- "They just don't care."

Often, educators create the facts that make their hypotheses come true. If the teacher believes that students don't want to learn, do want to cause trouble, are unmotivated, and don't care, then their students will live down to their teacher's expectations. Students sense positive regard from significant others. The more they feel valued, the harder they are likely to work.

Good and Brophy (1994) reported that teachers tend to treat low and high achievers differently based on their optimistic or pessimistic views regarding these students' likelihood of success. Teachers give low achievers less time to answer a question and more often criticize low achievers for failure. Teachers tend to give high achievers more eye contact and are friendlier, smile more, and give them more nonverbal signals of support. All these behaviors reflect optimism or pessimism.

It should to be pointed out, however, that the optimism we are emphasizing is not the belief that positive results are guaranteed if one just has positive thoughts. This is obviously naïve and unrealistic. What we are stressing is melioristic optimism, the idea that good things have a better chance of occurring if a person has a pragmatic openness to positive possibilities. Rutger Bregman (2020), in his book, *Humankind: A Hopeful History*, points out that this melioristic optimistic perspective works well in economics, politics, and education because there is good evidence "that most people, deep down, are pretty decent" (p. 2).

Intentionality

Educators today talk a lot about the importance of mindsets. Gary Klein (2016) defines mindset as "a belief that orients the way we handle situations—the way we sort out what is going on and what we should do" (p. 1). An invitational mindset is easily defined by the Five Assumptions of Invitational Education that were introduced in Chapter 1. Take a moment to review these statements and imagine using them as an invitational mindset to guide your choice of words and actions:

1. People are able, valuable, and responsible and should be treated accordingly.
2. Educating should be a collaborative, cooperative activity.
3. The process is the product in the making.
4. People possess untapped potential in all areas of worthwhile human endeavor.
5. This potential can best be realized by places, policies, programs, and processes specifically designed to invite development and by people who are intentionally inviting with themselves and others personally and professionally.

> By definition, an invitation is a purposive act. It is intended to offer something beneficial for consideration.

By definition, an invitation is a purposive act. It is intended to offer something beneficial for consideration. This definition suggests a purposive act intended to benefit the recipient.

The more intentionality the teacher can exhibit, the more accurate his or her judgments and the more decisive his or her behavior. An extreme example of intentionality is illustrated by a Hollywood agent who was told to get lost and "not come back for ten years." The agent responded: "Morning or afternoon?"

Another aspect of intentionality is that it helps teachers generate multiple choices in a given situation. Intentional individuals develop plans, act on many possible opportunities, and evaluate the effects of these actions. It takes intentionality to be inviting, particularly when facing obstacles, challenges, and apparent rejection. The value of intentionality is revealed in one student's successful change in behavior, as described by Purkey and Strahan (2002, pp. 14–15):

> Keith was one of those students "whose reputation preceded him" to the middle school. His elementary teachers passed along horror stories of his escapades; the day he inked his hands to leave a trail of blue prints along the white walls of his third-grade classroom, the time in fourth grade when he used his scissors to "trim" the hair of a girl seated in front of him, his record number of trips to the principal's office in fifth grade. According to records, his previous teachers had tried everything from conferring, consulting and confronting, to detention, demerits, and deterrents—all to no avail.
>
> When the sixth-grade teacher learned that Keith would be one of his students in the fall, he began to plan for success. Several weeks before the start of the school year he sent a card to all his incoming students (including a special note to Keith) welcoming them to his class. Next, he studied Keith's records and found not only an abundance of referrals but also a number of indications of academic potential.
>
> On the first day of class, students were asked to complete autobiographical inventories describing their interests. Keith listed "pets" and "reading" among his likes. When Keith interrupted class discussion with, "Hey, did you hear about the guy who tried to dry his cat in the microwave?" the teacher waved off his comment and moved closer to him. A second disruption was greeted by the teacher with "We will talk about this after class."
>
> During the private conference the teacher explained his expectations for the class and asked Keith to talk about his expectations as well. During the conference the teacher also asked Keith to help him set up a class aquarium. After the aquarium was operating, the teacher encouraged Keith to join several students as tutors in a reading program for younger students. Maintaining the aquarium and serving as a tutor helped Keith feel a part of the class and assisted him in improving his behavior. Keith acted up from time to time, but the teacher's intentional efforts were successful in improving the student's behavior.

In the situation with Keith, intentional invitational teaching is visible. The teacher worked to develop a relationship based on mutual trust and respect. The teacher was optimistic that Keith could learn self-discipline and was intentional with a plan of action. At its best, invitational teaching can overcome years of unruly student behavior. Chapter 5 will present ways to maintain an inviting stance in the face of major obstacles, challenges, and apparent rejection.

THE ACTIONS OF EDUCATORS

Earlier the idea was presented that each professional has the ability and responsibility to function in a professionally inviting manner. However, it is possible for a message, no matter how well-meaning, to be perceived as disinviting. Attractive or repellent qualities remain in the eyes of the beholder. There is no guarantee that the most well-intentioned actions will be viewed positively by others.

Numerous classification systems have been developed for categorizing messages. The classification system that fits the approach presented in this book involves the following four categories: Level One, intentionally disinviting; Level Two, unintentionally disinviting; Level Three, unintentionally inviting; and Level Four, intentionally inviting. These levels are an adaptation of Howell's (1982) conscious and unconscious "Levels of Competence."

Level One: Intentionally Disinviting

Acknowledging that some messages are meant to be disinviting is painful. Comments such as "Shut up," "I know you're not that stupid," "Why did you bother to come to school today?" and "Quit acting like a girl," fit into this level. Professionals functioning at the intentionally disinviting level are aware of the disabling, demeaning, and devaluing potential of their behavior. Exactly why some people choose to function at this bottom level is unclear. But regardless of the reasons—whether because of racial or gender prejudice, unrequited love, personal inadequacy, or negative self-image—if they are unable or unwilling to change, fellow professionals have the responsibility to caringly but firmly remove them from daily contact with students.

Fortunately, relatively few educators function at Level One for any extended period of time. Intentionally disinviting messages are usually communicated in fits of anger or frustration. A major problem with Level One behavior is that these intentionally disinviting actions tend to be justified by some individuals as being "good" for students. The authors of this book can think of no circumstances in which it is good to demean students or where a professional can justify intentionally disinviting behavior. Teachers who use sarcasm often defend their actions by claiming that students enjoy it. Even if the target of the teacher's sarcasm laughs it off, that should not be interpreted as enjoying being the subject of the joke. The student is likely laughing to save face in front of the other students. Sarcasm models intentionally disinviting behavior and has no place in schools.

Educators who seek to operate from an inviting stance have a responsibility to keep their schools on task.

Another form of intentionally disinviting behavior is exhibited by the person who sends mixed but predominantly disinviting messages. People who behave this way mean to be disinviting but may alter their behavior when confronted. For example, in the movie *On Golden Pond*, Norman (Henry Fonda) often exhibited disinviting behaviors, but when confronted in a serious and persistent way, he was willing to change. Sometimes such confrontation can be beneficial to those involved. If intentionally disinviting messages in schools go unchallenged, then schools may move away from their primary function—to invite human potential. Educators who seek to operate from an inviting stance have a responsibility to keep their schools on task.

A nonjudgmental way to begin the conversation about disinviting messages is to help school adults understand how strong negative emotions may trigger us to react without thinking. Dan Siegel (1999) explains that we all have a "Window of Tolerance" within which we can respond thoughtfully to the demands of life. However, when a situation is outside of our window of tolerance, we may become stressed, experience hyper-arousal, and lose our ability to think rationally. This may trigger us to react in a disinviting way. Teaching mindful practices to students and staff can help us notice when we are stressed and develop our ability to let the stressful feeling subside before choosing a response.

Level Two: Unintentionally Disinviting

A much larger problem in schools stems from the people, places, policies, programs, and processes that are unintentionally disinviting. Educators who operate at Level Two are typically well meaning, but their behavior is often seen by others as chauvinistic, racist, sexist, condescending, or simply thoughtless. Comments such as "What Earl is trying to say" and "It's easy, anyone can do it" typify this level. Professionals who function at Level Two spend a lot of time wondering "What did I do wrong?" "Why aren't my students learning more?" "Why is everyone so upset with me?"

Teaching that is unintentionally disinviting is often characterized by boredom, busywork, and insensitivity to feelings. Examples of such insensitivity appear again and again in student accounts of being disinvited: "I feel insulted when faculty sponsors always ask a female to take minutes," wrote one girl. Another student described how she was disinvited by a teacher who said: "You can try out for the part . . . if you really want to." A third student complained that the teacher always used the term "broken home" when he could just as easily have said "single-parent family." The actions of educators perceived by others as sexist, racist, patronizing, or thoughtless are likely to be interpreted as disinviting despite the educator's good intentions.

Level Three: Unintentionally Inviting

Educators functioning at Level Three seem to have stumbled into particular ways of functioning that are usually effective, but they have a difficult time explaining why this is so. As good as they are, they usually lack a consistent stance from which to operate. Many so-called natural-born teachers, those who may never have thought much about what they are doing, but who are effective in the classroom, are successful because they are functioning at Level Three. They typically behave in ways that result in student feelings of being invited, although the teachers are largely unaware of the dynamics involved.

Professionals who function at Level Three are like the early "barnstorming" airplane pilots. These pioneer pilots didn't know a lot about aerodynamics, weather patterns, or navigation. They flew by the "seats of their pants." As long as they stayed close to the ground and the weather was clear so they could follow the highways and railroad tracks, they did fine. When the weather turned ugly or night fell, however, they became disoriented and got lost. In difficult situations, they lacked a dependable guidance system and tended to regress to lower levels of functioning.

The problem with functioning at the unintentionally inviting level is that the educator can become disoriented and unable to identify the reasons for his or her successes or failures. If whatever "it" is should stop working, the teacher does not know how to start it up again or what changes to make in his or her behavior. In other words, the teacher lacks a consistent stance—a dependable position from which to operate. A colleague, Charles Branch, once remarked that he would rather work with people who are functioning at Level One than those who are at Level Three. At least with Level One you know where you stand. The need for consistency and dependability in professional relationships sets the stage for Level Four.

Level Four: Intentionally Inviting

Educators should strive to be intentionally inviting. Doing so requires understanding the reasons for and the results of one's behavior and having the desire to function in a dependably inviting manner. But even at this top level, some are more successful than others in their actions. Here are some possible reasons for degrees of success within the broad category of Level Four.

Educators who seek to be intentionally inviting, but who are uncertain about the process, are going through a transition period. (This transitional process is analyzed in Chapter 7, using the HELIX.) They begin to understand the processes involved and make a conscious effort to be inviting. When they face difficult situations, however, they may resort to lower and perhaps more familiar levels of functioning. Students generally feel good about these beginning Level Four teachers but may have a vague feeling that these teachers are not too dependable and can't be counted on in tough situations. With experience and practice, teachers are likely to move successfully through this transition period. Educators who are dependable in their actions consistently face diverse and difficult situations with a particular stance. The importance of consistency and dependability is illustrated in the following:

Stubborn Teacher

My teacher is so stubborn!
She is told that I am unmotivated. But she invites me anyway.
She is told that I don't want to learn. She invites me anyway.
She is told that I don't have the ability. She invites me anyway.
She is told I just want to cause trouble. She invites me anyway.
She invites me again, and again, and again.
She fills my world with invitations.
One day, I'll take the greatest risk of my life.
I'll accept one, and see what happens.

WWP

When educators who are functioning at Level Four perceive, choose, and act with consistency and sensitivity, they are likely to become artfully inviting. At this point educators have integrated Level Four behaviors into what appears to be an effortless, natural activity, but is actually the product of serious and sustained effort. The process is similar to that gone through by someone who has worked to become fluent enough in a language to think and create in it. Artfully inviting educators think in a special language of "doing with" rather than "doing to." They have developed the ability to approach even the most difficult situation in a professionally inviting manner. When educators who are functioning at this advanced level face problems, they can rely on their understanding of Invitational Education to develop solutions.

Educators functioning at Level Four are like modern commercial jet pilots. Thanks to their knowledge, they can "fly on instruments" around or over dangerous weather fronts. In the final analysis, this ability to chart and maintain a dependable flight pattern makes the difference between success or failure as a professional helper.

Recognition of the ability to be intentionally inviting and the artful use of this ability can be tremendous assets. By understanding the four levels of functioning, by seeking to function at the highest level, and by improving abilities within this level, educators can be powerful forces in inviting school success.

The Plus Factor

When people watch the accomplished musician, the headline comedian, the world-class athlete, the master teacher, what they are seeing seems simple. It is only when people try to do it themselves that they realize that true art requires painstaking care, discipline, and deliberate planning over extended periods of time.

At its best, the inviting approach becomes "invisible" because it becomes a means of addressing humanity. To borrow the words of Chuang-tse, a Chinese philosopher from the late 4th century, "It flows like water, reflects like a mirror, and responds like an echo." At its best, the inviting approach requires implicit, rather than explicit, expression. When the educator reaches this special plateau, the result appears effortless. Football teams call it "momentum," comedians call it "feeling the center," world class athletes call it "finding the zone," fighter pilots call it "rhythm." In invitational theory it is called the Plus Factor. A good example of this factor in action was provided by Ginger Rogers, the famous actress and dancer. When describing dancing with Fred Astaire, she said, "It's a lot of hard work, that I do know." Someone responded, "But it doesn't look it, Ginger." Ginger replied, "That's why it's magic." Invitational theory, at its best, works like magic. Those who function at the highest levels of inviting become so fluent over time that the carefully honed skills and techniques they employ are invisible to the untrained eye. They function with such talented assurance that the tremendous effort involved does not call attention to itself.

> *At its best, the inviting approach becomes "invisible" because it becomes a means of addressing humanity.*

SUMMARY

Because Invitational Education is both obvious and elusive it requires the artful blending of teacher perceptions, stance, and behaviors. This involves viewing students and oneself as able, valuable, and responsible and having a positive view of the educative process. Teacher stance represents the disposition of all school adults regarding trust, respect, optimism, and intentionality. These qualities are essential ingredients in creating and maintaining a socially and emotionally safe climate for everyone in schools.

Chapter 3 provided a simple classification procedure for evaluating personal and professional conduct: (a) intentionally disinviting, (b) unintentionally disinviting, (c) unintentionally inviting, (d) intentionally inviting. The next chapter presents the "craft" of Invitational Education, which includes being ready, doing with, following through, and the choices involved in making the inviting approach a viable theory of practice.

FURTHER REFLECTIONS AND ACTIVITIES

1. Children who live with undependable adults may not initially trust the positive actions of a well-meaning school adult, and might refuse your invitation to help them or give them a second chance to complete an assignment or retake a test. In "reading their behavior backwards," what might be the cause behind their behavior? What inviting words and actions can you use to gain that student's trust over time?

2. A large banner displayed over the central staircase in a middle school states: *"You've got to give respect to get respect."* In your opinion, does this statement reflect an invitational viewpoint? Why or why not?

3. Imagine that a colleague of yours is consistently successful with their usual teaching strategy. One day, when the usual approach does not work with a student, the teacher feels frustrated and insulted and blames the student. What might you say in response to your colleague's feelings and behavior?

CHAPTER 4

The Skills of Inviting Educators

> The best teacher is one who, through establishing a personal relation, frees
> the student to learn. Learning can only take place in the student, and the
> teacher can only create the conditions for learning. The atmosphere created
> by a good interpersonal relationship is the major condition for learning.
> (Patterson, 1973, p. 98)

Obviously, all educators are inviting from time to time, either intentionally
or unintentionally. However, those who are perceived by others as dependably inviting possess two vital characteristics. First, they "hold the point"
like champion birddogs. That is, they consistently function in an inviting
manner, even in the most difficult and challenging situations. They reflect
unconditional respect for the value, ability, and self-directing powers of
those with whom they work. Second, they creatively integrate a variety of
skills into the craft of inviting. This chapter looks at a sequence of skills and
their artful orchestration to better assist educators in developing this craft.

Invitational Education involves blending perception and stance into
those activities that are most appropriate for the varied situations in which
professionals find themselves. Although no two situations are ever the same,
there are skills that inviting educators can use before, during, and after interactions with students and others. These skills are of special value in creating and sustaining more humane schools.

Some cautionary words are necessary when considering craft as the integration of skills. Being intentionally inviting results from basic perceptions
regarding oneself, others, and the world and from developing and maintaining an inviting stance. When offering something beneficial for consideration,
it is necessary to see the process as fluid. Things may change during the
process, even the nature of the invitation. It is vital to pay attention to the
purposes of everyone involved.

The skills described in this chapter cannot be applied mindlessly and me-
chanically to every situation because they are not techniques to move people
in desired directions like functionaries in a system. Rather, these skills are
principled strategies for developing doing-with relationships. Skills are aids
for ethical persuasion and not tools for manipulation. Significant harm can
be done by people who have learned the techniques and skills of Invitational

> *Significant harm can be done by people who have learned the techniques and skills of Invitational Education but who lack an understanding of the basic assumptions of an inviting theory of practice.*

Education but who lack an understanding of the basic assumptions of an inviting theory of practice. Without this understanding, there is always the danger that techniques can replace dialogue in the interpersonal process. This would be the antithesis of Invitational Education.

Although techniques can easily be over-emphasized, several skills can be valuable to educators. These skills can be learned and improved upon. In an inviting school, teachers have more rather than fewer skills and as a result have more degrees of freedom in working with people. Skills are both useful in themselves as well as a means of systematically developing deeper understandings and more integrated behaviors. The following are three clusters of skills: those associated with being ready, doing with, and following through.

BEING READY

The Scouts BSA motto "Be Prepared" is a good beginning for developing inviting skills. Being ready helps prevent being overwhelmed and sets the tone for what follows. Two aspects of being ready are preparing the environment and preparing oneself.

Preparing the Environment

The moment anyone arrives on the school grounds, or even the moment that anyone makes contact with the school, a mental image of the school is formed. The school environment is where students develops their positive or negative attitudes about learning and about themselves as learners. Students receive constant signals from the physical settings of schools, signals that tell them how much the people who design, build, operate, maintain, and manage schools care about them and their learning. For example, one student, describing her school, put it this way: "Yuk! How would you like to spend your whole day in a place that looks like this?" Sadly, teachers sometimes say the same thing.

Preparing an inviting environment involves creating a clean, comfortable, and safe setting in which people who work in schools feel welcome and at ease. Everything in the school counts. Developing an optimal physical environment means working to ensure that rooms, hallways, and commons areas are adequately cleaned, lighted, and heated; have plenty of fresh air, comfortable furniture, living plants, attractive bulletin boards; and are freshly painted. An often overlooked, but particularly disinviting aspect of schools can be noisy, fluorescent lights that keep buzzing in your head, even after you leave the room.

Adequate supplies are also important, as one teacher explained in this vignette: "One of my five-year-olds is left-handed. Last week I overheard a discussion he had with another student over the importance of having left-handed scissors and cutting well. He then proceeded to ask, 'Mrs. Mancino didn't you buy those left-handed scissors just for me?'" Even left-handed scissors can be a special invitation.

Educators who understand and practice Invitational Education find ways to improve the physical environment, even when "nothing can be done about the problem." From an inviting point of view, something can always be done. Challenging defeatist and often self-fulfilling statements is a good beginning. For example, state regulations often require the posting of warning notices regarding entering the building and where to report. Sometimes the wording is less than inviting in nature. School officials might consider using the required language and adding a positive comment below. A beneficial exercise for your staff might be to examine all the signs that are in their classrooms and hallways to determine how someone might perceive the stated messages. Are the directives threatening or inviting? Staff and perhaps students can suggest ways to revise them. Recognizing how we interpret messages will help us become more conscious of how messages we send to others might be received.

> *Those who practice Invitational Education find innovative ways to break out of lock-step methods in creating and operating schools.*

People both create and are created by their environments. By that we mean people develop standardized practices for meeting their needs but get locked into the mindset of these practices: The tools control the workers. Things are done without thought because that is how they have always been done. Those who practice Invitational Education find innovative ways to break out of lock-step methods in creating and operating schools.

An excellent example of a physically inviting school is Lancashire Elementary School in Wilmington, Delaware. Just a few things former principal Fred Michaels and his staff have done include constructing a large sign welcoming everyone to the school, planting a tree inside the school, making one hallway into a cave museum, having students bring bricks and build their own road in a side corridor, and decorating the teachers' lounge so that it looks better than most restaurants. Even with these accomplishments, Fred Michaels often said, "We've only just begun!" Other examples of physically inviting schools include the historic Celoron Elementary School in Celoron, New York. Principal Charlie Brown organized parents, and together they dug a beautiful swimming pool in the basement of the 60-year-old school. In the Jiangsu Province of mainland China, the Nanjing Hanzhongmen Primary School teachers, students, and parents worked together to create an inviting campus. A pond with more than 1,000 golden carp greets you at the school gate. Students record and write stories about the majestic Great Grandfather Tree, play the piano in the hall, plant vegetables and grain in the Happy Farm, and enjoy beautiful student paintings.

Lancashire, Celoron, and Nanjing Hanzhongmen schools are creative illustrations of people preparing the environment to develop the most inviting place in town.

Preparing Oneself

Becoming an inviting educator involves recollecting and reflecting on what it was like to be an invited, or disinvited student. Inviting educators can deepen their experiential base by recalling specific instances in which they were invited, others in which they were disinvited, then answering these questions: "What happened?" "How did I feel?" "How do I feel now reflecting on this incident?" "What would I change?" "What inviting and disinviting experiences might students in my classroom be sharing 20 years from now?" Making Invitational Education personal and concrete removes it from the realm of abstract theory and moral exhortation and assists educators in remembering what it was like when they were on the student's side of the desk.

Educators can prepare themselves to be inviting to everyone in the school, especially those with different backgrounds, by examining their own suppositions. One of the most important things that educators can do is become aware of their own biases toward and stereotypes about certain others, thus recognizing the influence of these perceptions on the academic performance of students.

Inviting skills are more likely to be successful when educators are honest with themselves about their own feelings and work to remove negative ones. Martin Haberman (1994) developed a five-step process that educators can use in addressing their own prejudices.

First, he asks educators to survey their belief systems and list those individuals and groups that they believe to be inferior (for example, people of other races, people whose sexual identity differs from their own, people who are poor, or people who have disabilities). For those educators who go into denial ("I have no prejudices . . . what sort of person do you think I am?"), the likelihood is that they will not move from this stance. In such cases, their roles as educators are jeopardized. They are unable to face themselves and they become questionable company for young people.

Second, Haberman asks educators to inquire about the sources of their prejudices: "Where did I learn these things, from whom, when, and under what circumstances?"

Third, educators should ask themselves: "In what ways do I personally benefit from my prejudices?" For example, if I am wealthy, do I benefit from tax shelters at the expense of others? If I am of the dominant religious faith, do I benefit from restricting the rights of other religions or the areligious? This third step is particularly revealing, for it demonstrates how society may encourage certain prejudices.

Fourth, educators need to examine how prejudices influence what individuals hold to be true about children, teaching, learning, and the educative process. Questions to be considered here include attitudes toward tracking, grouping, retention, promotion, penalties, punishments, and the nature of the curriculum. What biases exist regarding gender, race, sexual orientation, age, or socioeconomic or ethnic background?

The fifth and final step according to Haberman, is to encourage educators to work out a definite plan to check prejudices, challenge them, and move beyond them.

Educators who wish to be inviting work at assessing their biases and seek ways in which they can develop greater respect for individual differences and cultural diversity. Some ways of accomplishing this include attending workshops and cultural festivals and participating in various human relations programs. The result may be greater sensitivity and selectivity in choosing curriculum material. The result may also be more appropriate and caring phrases, examples, jokes, and stories used in the classroom, teachers' lounge, conference center, or wherever professionals gather. Another approach is to get to know someone in your school or a family with a background different from your own. Even a 30-minute conversation over lunch can provide new insights and perspectives to help us enjoy and value people simply for who they are as individuals. With such opportunities available for educating oneself, there is no justification for professionals to remain uninformed.

> *Educators who seek to be strictly objective in dealing with students are operating from an educationally distorted position.*

Educators who seek to be inviting in our multicultural society can systematically deal with curricular and cultural transformation. Arguing that a subtle but persistent monocultural undertone is disinviting in process and consequences to an ever-growing portion of the school population, they can urge fellow educators to become advocates for multicultural reform. In the fight against prejudices, teachers cannot be neutral spectators. They should be combatants against the subtle and not so subtle forces that negate the worth and ability of any of their students between and within cultures. Using the insights of Ruby Payne (2018), educators can fight the cultural practices of a school or community that get students to feel less than or separate from others in the school community.

Educators who seek to be strictly objective in dealing with students are operating from an educationally distorted position. To merely be objective is to make an object of that which is being studied. Students are more than objects and teachers more than cataloguers. As human beings who seek to make a life in a world that might negate their background, culture, and basic worth, students can be supported by teachers who are on their side and who sense what they experience. Being ready means to proactively deal with realizing the ability, value, and responsibilities of every student.

BEING WITH

Being inviting is a special way of interacting with people. After preparing the environment and themselves, educators who desire to be personally and professionally inviting work to develop the following seven skills: (1) developing trust, (2) reaching each student, (3) reading situations, (4) making invitations attractive, (5) ensuring delivery, (6) negotiating, and (7) handling rejection.

Developing Trust

The importance of developing trust in schools has been documented for decades. Nel Noddings (1984, 1993, 2005) has stressed the importance of students perceiving that they are understood, received, respected, and recognized by teachers. In particular, she emphasizes that teachers demonstrate full receptivity to the other and the furthering of the other's purposes. What better way to encourage safety in schools than to have a student body that trusts its teachers and who will come to them and report potential dangers? It is hard to trust people who seem distracted and only concerned about themselves.

In addition, educators develop trust by using nonjudgmental language, respecting a student's confidentiality, and following through on agreements. One betrayal of trust can destroy the best relationship. This was expressed to us by a graduate student: "When I was in high school, I went to my football coach and shared my feelings about a personal matter. He seemed to listen and respect what I had to say, but at the next practice he kept bringing it up in front of the other guys. I'll never forgive him for that." Once a confidence is violated, it is difficult to reestablish a trusting relationship.

Trust is communicated by a person's entire body. Many researchers have provided ample evidence that we constantly communicate deeper feelings with the language of behavior. Every verbal message (for example, "Welcome to the 5th grade") also has a behavioral message. The nonverbal message may lie in the teacher's tone of voice, physical appearance, body stance, facial expression, gestures, and physical proximity. Eye contact—looking directly at a particular student—especially can signal, "I am sincere in what I say, and my welcome is especially for you." A warm tone of voice, a neat physical appearance, a friendly smile, and direct eye contact all communicate that the student really is welcome. On the other hand, a teacher's aloof behavior, forced smile, tightly crossed arms, or indifferent manner may say more clearly than words, "I would rather not be here with you."

Nonverbal language is so important that a hallmark of inviting educators is that they ensure their eye contact, body posture, facial expression, and tone of voice agree with their verbal messages. They appear serious when stating displeasure, they look at another person when expressing sincerity, and they tense their bodies when expressing frustration. Their body language agrees with their spoken language, even in complex situations.

Because others are quick to spot conflicts between what teachers say and how they behave, it is vital for inviting educators to "come on straight." Coming on straight means sharing feelings of happiness, anger, enthusiasm, sadness, excitement, or boredom. Teachers who can express their feelings are more likely to be seen as "real" by students. One high school student expressed the importance of real behavior by a teacher with these words: "I remember that our high school history teacher was not afraid to express his feelings. He let us know when our misbehavior was getting to him. But he didn't show just his angry side. Once he cried at the end of a movie shown in class when the hero died. I learned a lot from him besides history . . . that it's OK for a man to express an emotion besides anger."

Coming on straight does not mean unbridled self-disclosure. Although self-disclosure and sharing one's feelings with others can be important, such sharing should not be overdone. Disclosure should be relevant to the nature of the relationship and appropriate to the situation. When others casually ask about one's situation, they do not expect a complete medical history. Accepting and applying an inviting approach does not consist of displaying one's every immediate emotion. Just because you may feel like being intentionally disinviting does not mean you should be. In other words, coming on straight means taking the total situation into account when displaying feelings, and choosing behaviors that are caring and appropriate to the circumstances.

Self-disclosure is also determined by how comfortable each individual is about revealing himself or herself to others. People vary in how much they choose to share. Some teachers are more open than others. It is important, therefore, that teachers take their own feelings into account when determining how much of themselves they choose to share and how skilled they will be in the process. At times this may mean letting others know when and why they are uncomfortable about something.

Perhaps the best way to summarize the importance of being real with students is to quote a teacher: "During the real 'up tight' period of the school year following Christmas vacation, I found a note under my classroom door. It read: 'Mr. Maggor, be yourself, don't try to be someone you're not.' It was signed 'A student and a friend.' Suddenly I realized that I had been coming down hard and mean on little things, which was not me and not my usual behavior. Later the two students, neither of whom I had in class, stopped by and talked with me about it. That day I learned a lot about the importance of being myself with my students."

Reaching Each Student

Simply sending inviting messages is not enough. Invitations are a means for personally involving each student in his or her education. Teachers who practice Invitational Education ensure that their invitations to learning are distributed fairly and sensitively and are received and acknowledged by each student. Teachers tend to communicate a disproportionate number of invitations to some students while neglecting others. The problem of favoritism, exclusion,

School safety depends heavily on educators reaching out to students who are choosing behaviors that isolate themselves from school adults and peers.

and their negative influences on both self-concept and school achievement is self-evident. This is particularly important in reaching and helping students with emotional problems such as anger.

Troubled students will usually give warning signs of their mounting anger. They typically withdraw from friendships and school activities. They might withdraw by being negatively different. They will use anything that will create a barrier and tell the world "I don't care." When students feel that no one likes them, cares about them, or respects them, they begin to think that they don't like, care, or respect others. Such feelings could set the stage for a terrible tragedy. School safety depends heavily on educators reaching out to students who are choosing behaviors that isolate themselves from school adults and peers. While it may be easier to ignore a student who appears angry and not interested in your attention, it is this student who needs you most.

In classrooms, one way to reduce or eliminate favoritism is to send learning invitations systematically. Rather than relying on a random pattern of interaction in which the teacher will most likely call on those students perceived as having the correct answer, the inviting teacher works to ensure that each student is summoned cordially to participate in class. This is accomplished through rotating assignments, seating charts, class rosters, check sheets, card files, or other means of insuring that each student is given an equal opportunity to respond and comment during instruction. The teacher's attention is equally spread out, and time is taken for some personal contact with each student each day.

The importance of the time reserved for one-on-one contacts with individual students cannot be overestimated. Although not easy with large classes, it is vital that the teacher squeeze in a few moments for semiprivate chats. These chats (sometimes referred to as check-ins) may last less than a minute, but they can be powerful incentives to learning. Inviting teachers use odd bits and pieces of time for these brief talks (while waiting for the bell, walking to the car, serving on lunchroom or playground duty, straightening up after class, or storing equipment). This habit of reaching out to all students is particularly helpful to ensure connection with quiet, submissive, subdued students who can easily be overlooked or ignored.

One high school teacher who had several large classes said he developed a weekly plan for reaching each of his students. He took the number of students in each class, divided by five, selected that number of students and made sure he made some personal contact with each of them that day. By the end of the week he had made some personal communication with each student in his classes. He said this system pointed out to him that there were students he would have otherwise missed, and it also gave him a more balanced perspective about what was happening in his classroom and in the lives of his students.

At the Joe Stanley Smith Elementary School in Carlsbad, New Mexico, every student in the school receives a brief one-on-one check-in with a teacher every day, to discover how their day went and what they might need help with. Small, mixed-class learning groups on each grade level are then reorganized frequently. Teachers plan together and regularly teach each other's students in these personalized learning groups. This does much more than ensure that all learning needs are addressed promptly. It messages the students that all teachers in their school are committed to helping them realize their potential.

Another way to interact systematically with students is through written correspondence. Whether the teacher calls the process journals, letters, notes, or insight cards, encouraging students to write regular messages of some sort to the teacher is helpful. These messages might consist of questions, frustrations, reactions, arguments, comments, complaints, or suggestions. Their purpose is to open up a system of written communication between the teacher and each student. Of course, respect for confidentiality and professional ethics should be followed when asking students to self-disclose. The teacher can also send brief, written messages to the students by responding to their notes. Teachers who use this system report that some students who rarely speak in class become eloquent when encouraged to present their thoughts in written notes.

The value of systematic patterns of classroom interaction is significant. When teachers call on students to read in a patterned instead of random way, so that students know in advance the reading order, stress among anxiety-prone students is reduced, and excessive competition (a consider-able problem among high socioeconomic status children) is lessened.

One further way to reach each student and to call forth student achieve-ment is to demonstrate a purposeful intentional attitude. Students are more likely to accept invitations to learning when they perceive the teacher as being organized, competent, and prepared for class. When inviting students to partake in a learning experience or task that they might not be interested in, Deci (1995) suggests providing a rationale for why the new information or requested task is of value, acknowledging the students' feelings about the activity, and using a style of language that involves minimal pressure.

Reading Situations

To emphasize the importance of reading situations, Aesop tells in one of his fables how the fox is able to cross the thin ice of a pond while other animals, even those who weigh less than the fox, fall through the ice and drown. The fox's secret is that it listens to the sound of the ice. Classroom teachers some-times fail to listen to the sounds of students. They react without taking the time to hear what students are saying. Such teacher behavior was described by a junior high school student who wrote: "My science teacher tries to be a good teacher, but he never listens to anyone. One day I sat next to him in assembly and he asked me how I was doing. I told him that I had a terrible headache. He replied, 'Fine, fine, fine.' He didn't hear a word I said."

Reading situations is the process whereby the teacher attends carefully to students to understand how his or her invitations to learning are be-ing received, interpreted, and acted upon. Various terms have been used to describe this process over the years, including "active listening" (Gordon, 1974), "resonating with the client" (Rogers, 1967), and "attending" (Egan, 1990). Perhaps the blinded Gloucester in Shakespeare's *King Lear* described the process best when he said, "I see it feelingly" (4.6.152). But whatever term is used, this is the process teachers use to understand what is occurring within the stu-dent's perceptual world. This calls for *reading behavior backwards,* looking beyond the stu-dent's overt behavior to what that behavior in-dicates about the student's internal world. For example, a student's bitter complaint of help-lessness over an assigned problem may mean that the student is feeling frustration or feels a lack of competence and is asking for reassurance. This skill of reading behavior backwards is so important that training educators to understand how things seem from another person's viewpoint should be a major goal of teacher education programs.

> *In the final analysis, each individual is the world's greatest authority on himself or herself. Only the person with the pain knows where it hurts.*

In the final analysis, each individual is the world's greatest authority on himself or herself. Only the person with the pain knows where it hurts. For teachers, this means that their invitations are invariably perceived by students in the light of the students' past experiences. To be asked to wash the chalkboard may be viewed as inviting by one child, but definitely disinviting by another. No two individuals ever share exactly the same past, and no two students ever perceive a teacher's invitation in the same way. To predict the likelihood of an invitation being accepted by a student, one first develops sensitivity to how that message might appear and sound in the eyes and ears of the beholder.

Here is an example of how things appear differently when seen from an internal point of view: "Some years ago I had a high school student who appeared to be very poised and self-confident and who played the guitar with marvelous skill," wrote a teacher. "Yet we could never get him to accept our invitation to perform in public. Other teachers said it was because he felt superior to others in the school. But one day he confided in me that he would dearly love to perform, but stage fright made him physically sick with fear." The skill of listening with care helps teachers understand the personal world of students.

Reading situations also enables teachers to see beyond the games students play. Students fear failure much more than most teachers realize. In trying to avoid failure and the resulting embarrassment, students develop entire repertoires of behavior to convince teachers that they are learning when, in fact, they are not. Such repertoires include body stance (leaning forward), eye contact (steady gaze), nonverbal behavior (head nodding), and other activities (note-taking, question-asking, and so on). Students also learn that a successful way to respond when they do not think they can answer a question is to delay, hem and haw, or mumble. Even thinly veiled flattery sometimes misleads teachers into thinking that learning is taking place and that students feel good about themselves as learners. That these practices are commonplace is evidenced by research indicating that teacher ratings of students' self-concept-as-learner are significantly higher and more positive than the ratings students give themselves on the same scale (Harper & Purkey, 1993).

In the classroom, students learn early how to pull the wool over teachers' eyes. Many teachers are aware of such ploys. Indeed, they may have used some of them when they were students! Teachers who adopt an inviting approach use a variety of informal, nonthreatening evaluation techniques and discussions to determine what types of invitations to learning may be necessary and which ones are most likely to be accepted.

Attending to feedback and making the necessary adjustments is an important part of reading situations. This means that inviting educators are alert to the faintest signal from others that might indicate their desire to respond to an invitation: clearing of a throat, leaning forward, hand half raised, eye contact, or lingering after class. Successful teachers are aware of such positive nonverbal signals and take special responsibility for encouraging acceptance. They also take responsibility for doing everything possible to ensure that students who accept their invitations to learning have a good chance of success, for they understand that failing, after taking the risk of accepting an invitation, can have long-lasting negative effects.

Our colleague Mike Fagan described teacher efforts to maximize chances of student success this way: "An inviting teacher is like a good quarterback in football. When the quarterback throws a pass to a moving receiver, he tries to 'read the situation' and hit the receiver in full stride to maximize his motion, to get into the energy flow of the receiver and to move with him instead of trying to redirect him." By listening for clues in the variations of student behavior, inviting teachers can get into the flow of student energy, so chances of misunderstanding are minimized, and chances of success are enhanced.

Making Invitations Acceptable

Not all invitations are created equal. Dependably inviting teachers are aware of this and use this awareness to design and send messages that have a good chance of being accepted. These messages include body language (smiles, winks, and nods) and oral communication (statements that convey appreciation and express affirmation). Factors such as vocal manner, physical space, teacher appearance, and body language all have a significant impact on the communicative process.

Making invitations attractive does not mean that they have to be sugarcoated. Judy Stillion, our colleague, provided this example: "Imagine going to a party where the host offered you a piece of candy, then a jelly doughnut, next a piece of fudge, then a sugar cookie, and finally a cup of sweetened tea to wash it down! This would be hard to stomach." Inviting processes should be as well-balanced as nutritious meals; they should provide a variety of tastes and flavors—sweet, bitter, salty, and sour. Too much of one thing, even a good thing, can be disinviting. This especially applies to compliments and praise.

Invitations most likely to be accepted and acted upon successfully tend to be appropriate for the situation, are specific enough to be understood, and are not overly demanding.

Praise, for example, should be based on honest performance. Praise generally produces increases in effort, but compliments tossed out to students with little or no justification quickly lose all meaning. One student referred to his teacher as a "dead cat teacher": "If you brought her a dead cat, she would praise it." Many young people simply tune out the frequent verbal praise of adults, a result probably due to the unrealistic amount of praise distributed by some educators.

Muller and Dweck (1998) found that the type of praise students received influenced their mindset about intelligence. Students praised for their intelligence were more likely to develop a fixed mindset. They came to believe that they had a set amount of intelligence or ability that could not be changed. This led them to enjoy doing things that came easily to them and to lose interest or blame others when tasks are more challenging. To a person with a fixed mindset, failure is an indication of inability and can lead to a feeling of helplessness. On the other hand, praising students for their effort and the process they used when working on a task tended to nurture a growth mindset. They believed that with effort and experience you can grow your level of skill and intelligence. Growth-minded folks value effort, crave challenge, and persist in the face of obstacles. To them, failure is not an indication of inability, but simply a signal to change strategies and put forth more effort. To nurture growth mindsets, Dweck (2006) encourages teachers and parents to praise effort and the choice of strategies and process, rather than remark on how smart or talented the student is.

Invitations most likely to be accepted and acted upon successfully tend to be appropriate for the situation, are specific enough to be understood, and are not overly demanding. A colleague, Bruce Voelkel, pointed out that a limited-time invitation may be especially useful to educators. An example of a limited-time invitation would be a teacher saying to a colleague, "I have only ten minutes before I must attend a meeting, but meanwhile, let's go have a cup of coffee." Such an invitation lets the other person know that they do not have to invest a great deal of time and thus makes the invitation easier to accept.

Ensuring Delivery

Invitations are like letters—some get lost in the mail. Unless they are received, they do not count. People cannot accept invitations they have never received. Educators who are dependably inviting check to see that their invitations are received and acknowledged. Their messages are like registered mail—special steps are taken to ensure delivery.

A good example of the importance of confirmation of messages is provided by the U. S. Navy. Any message must be acknowledged for it to be considered received. The captain of a ship will order, "Flank speed." The engineer will confirm that the message has been received by replying, "Message received, flank speed."

Not only is acknowledgment vital in the U.S. Navy, it is also necessary in everyday living. How often have we complained about a wedding gift sent but not acknowledged? Perhaps the answer is in the dead-letter office of the U.S. Postal Service, where countless packages without proper addresses are auctioned. It is perfectly acceptable to ask, "Did you receive my wedding gift?" The recipient may not like your gift, but you have the right to know that is was received.

A good way to ensure delivery is through clarity. Clear, direct invitations are far more likely to be recognized and acted upon than vague or indirect ones. An invitation asking, "Please come for dinner on Saturday evening, October 22, at 8:00 P.M." has a better chance of acceptance than one saying, "Let's get together sometime." In addition, a specific invitation makes it easier for students to recognize and acknowledge invitations: "Mark, what did I ask you to do?" If the teacher's invitation is acknowledged, but still not accepted, at least the cards are on the table. The teacher is now in a better position to understand the situation. Did nonacceptance mean rejection, or does the student need time to consider? If the invitation was rejected, why? How can it be made acceptable? If it cannot be made acceptable, then what alternate invitations might lead to the desired results? By ensuring delivery, the teacher can make many choices apparent.

Checking the receipt of invitations is also important because in certain situations people do not know how to respond or cannot respond appropriately. Sometimes in classrooms, students would like to accept an invitation to learning but feel unable to do so. Because of self-doubt ("How could I ever learn this stuff?"), threat ("I'm afraid I'll look stupid if I try"), hostility ("They just want to make fun of me"), fear of disappointing others ("I'm not sure I can live up to her expectations"), or resignation ("I know I can't do math"), many students have difficulty in responding to even the most attractive invitations. Knowing this, dependably inviting teachers are patient in their work and do not give up easily. They make sure that their invitations are received and acknowledged. Ensuring delivery is particularly important when working with at-risk students.

Students will sometimes perceive the teacher's invitations in unusual ways. What is sent is not always what is received. The same encouragement may have sharply different meanings to different children, even children of the same age. The shy, insecure child may experience great anxiety at a teacher's invitation to read a story in front of the class. A child with high self-assurance may find the same invitation very appealing. Children with severe behavioral difficulties, or children filled with feelings of anger and frustration, may find acceptance of the most well-meaning invitations from teachers or peers very difficult. One teacher described such a student this way: "Tracy comes to school each day with hands clenched tightly, face in a frown. Nothing ever seems to go right for him. The least thing a child does to him will definitely end in a fight. His peers are always cheating him when playing games. The teacher has never liked him. The work is too hard. He leaves school each day with hands clenched tightly, face in a frown." Needless to say, Tracy is a challenge.

Children like Tracy are likely to hide their innermost feelings, and a teacher's invitations to feel able, valuable, and responsible may appear to be the last things they want. But inviting teachers are not misled. They understand that students who hold negative feelings about themselves face a great risk when they accept a teacher's invitation because they become vulnerable to further hurt. They also understand that, for students who have been consistently disinvited, a handful of invitations will seldom be enough to make an observable difference in behavior. Inviting teachers recognize the problems involved, yet they continue to believe their consistent efforts are worthwhile. Understanding the importance of persistence, they invite again and again and again, filling the classroom with invitations, then checking that these messages are received, acknowledged, and perhaps acted upon.

A former elementary school teacher who is the daughter of one of the authors, provided an example of the value of persistence. This daughter is an excellent teacher, but she almost met her match with "Mary." Mary was a foster child who had been terribly mistreated by life. Her situation was so intense that if the teacher so much as looked at Mary, the child would likely "go ballistic."

Day after day the young teacher, almost in tears, would talk to her father: "Dad, you know that Invitational Education stuff you teach, well, it's not working with Mary!" Week after week went by with little or no success with Mary, and week after week the author encouraged his young teacher to keep inviting. Week after week, he kept hearing, "Dad, Mary lost it again today."

On the last day of school, Mary waited until the other children departed, then brought a beat-up Valentine's Day candy box, in the shape of a heart, up to the teacher's desk, placed it down without a word, and walked out the door. The teacher opened the box (rather gingerly), and inside was a scrawled note, "To the best teacher in the world. Signed, Mary." In some cases, invitational teaching is an act of hope.

Negotiating

Invitational Education is a cooperative, collaborative activity that involves the participation of both the sender and the receiver. The sender determines the rules under which invitations are sent; the receiver determines the rules of acceptance. These rules are negotiable. For example, the principal might say, "Nancy, I would like you to help me decorate the stage for tomorrow's assembly." Nancy replies, "I can't come right now, but I'll come after my conference with a student." The negotiation is successfully concluded when the principal says, "Fine, I'll be looking for you after your conference." Willingness to negotiate is an important part of Invitational Education and an essential part of the democratic tradition.

In seeking acceptance of a request, inviting educators can subtly communicate, "Will you accept? If not now, when? If not this invitation, which one?" Willingness to negotiate is most important, because some people will not accept an invitation when first offered, just to see if the teacher really means it. Nel Noddings (2005) notes that children who live with undependable adults often mistrust school adults and don't believe the teacher is offering opportunities for their benefit. The teacher may need to invite them numerous times to demonstrate that they truly care about the individual, and not just the assignment or project. Inviting teachers do not give up easily. They are consistent and dependable in their stance.

Negotiating is not the simple repetition of the same invitation in the same way, over and over, like a broken record. As Walter Barbe commented in a personal communication, "If you've told a child something a thousand times, and the child still has not learned, then it is not the child who is the slow learner." The rejection of an invitation is one indication that the message may benefit by being amended and resubmitted.

Recognizing that an invitation to learning has been rejected, a teacher might ask the student, "If you won't accept this invitation, what invitation will you accept?" The purpose of negotiation from an invitational perspective is to seek a "doing-with" rather than a "doing-to" environment.

Many teachers at various levels have discovered the value of a contract grading system. Students contract for a particular grade to be earned on the basis of the work they help choose and promise to perform. Chemistry teacher Angela Campbell (2017) creates guided practices for her students, to help them master each unit objective in a low-risk environment. Students strive to earn at least a 70 on the summative assessment, which allows them to complete additional practices to further raise their score. The students who score 60 or lower are required to do even more practice, so they quickly learn to put the effort in to reach a 70. The feeling of competence inspires them to repeat the practice cycle and score even higher.

> Negotiating is the process of "getting to yes." This involves operating from a principled position and having available a wide variety of choices that coincide with the mutual interests of all involved.

Another approach might offer the student choices among alternatives that are made as appealing as possible: "You may choose to study vocabulary in small groups, or you may play a word recognition game." This confronts the student with firm expectations within a framework of respect. A student who is given a choice as to how to complete an assignment is more likely to follow through.

Negotiating is the process of "getting to yes." This involves operating from a principled position and having available a wide variety of choices that coincide with the mutual interests of all involved. This most certainly is a "doing-with" process. Even in the best of negotiations, however, there is no guarantee that an invitation will be accepted, no matter how attractively it is designed or artfully it is presented. That is because inviting is a dialogical and not a mechanical process. This introduces the skill of handling rejection.

Handling Rejection

Today the majority of educators are well trained and concerned with the welfare of others. They may be found in schools that reflect a commitment to learning and respect for feelings. Some educators, however, find themselves in less fortunate situations, swamped with assignments that appear to have little relevance to education. These include locker checks, hall-monitoring, money collecting, recordkeeping, playground supervision, lunchroom patrol, bus duty, and a host of other assignments. Teachers could more easily accept such duties if these responsibilities were not coupled with overcrowded classes, dilapidated facilities, apparently bored and apathetic colleagues, out-of-touch bureaucracies, and, perhaps most painful, disinterested and even hostile students who seem to reject the most well-intentioned invitations. (Later chapters will discuss ways to address these situations.)

Faced with numerous rejections, the teacher can easily become disillusioned, bitter, dejected, and may begin to think: "Why should I continue to invite students? My invitations are not accepted. Besides, they're not listed in our behavioral objectives, exit skills, or learning outcomes!" When this thinking takes over, another potentially great teacher joins the ranks of teachers living a professional half-life. This loss of hope and idealism is a terrible blow to education as well as a major calamity for the teacher. Such tragedies need not happen. When educators operate with patience and courage, conserving and focusing limited energies at the most effective times, they will not be easily intimidated and overwhelmed by what seem like impossible situations, in which their finest invitations are apparently rejected.

It is essential, first, for educators to consider whether or not their invitations have *in fact*, been rejected. Nonacceptance is not the same as rejection. Even an outright rejection of an invitation may be just the opposite. For example, one beginning teacher invited a student to help him move some supplies after class. "Are you kidding?" the student responded. "I got more important things to do." The teacher was hurt and resentful because he assumed that his invitation had been rudely rejected. Later, he was startled when the student showed up to help. Students accept or reject invitations in their own ways and on their own terms. It is important to understand that acceptances come in many forms. The person extending an invitation determines *what* is presented and *how*, but the person receiving the invitation determines *how* it will be acted upon, and *when*.

Even when an invitation is definitely, unmistakably, absolutely, and without question rejected, it is useful to separate the rejection from the person. Just because a student rejects an invitation does not mean that the student is rejecting the teacher. Students are not so much against others as for themselves. Students may reject, accept, or place invitations on hold for countless reasons that have absolutely nothing to do with the teacher.

One of the most common reasons for rejecting an invitation is the memory of similar invitations accepted in the past but found less than satisfying. If past invitations have resulted in failure, embarrassment, or humiliation, it is a great risk to accept present ones. Teachers who understand this process are less likely to blame themselves or consider it a personal insult when their invitations are rejected. These teachers head back to the drawing board to develop more appropriate invitations. They are not dismayed, and they are not resigned.

Beyond the psychological reasons for rejecting invitations, there are also environmental reasons. The physical conditions of the classroom and school, lighting, public address system, class size, temperature, general aesthetics, scheduling, and even class makeup of students with varying backgrounds, gender, race, socioeconomic levels, and ranges of achievement—all these contribute to acceptance or rejection.

It is important to remember that everything makes a difference. Even the smallest and subtlest and most seemingly insignificant factors can have a profound influence on how we see ourselves, others, and the world. Often the little things in life have the greatest influence. Any invitation, no matter how small or in what area, has tremendous potential. What appears to be a trifle can, in the right situation, make a significant difference. Teachers have an excellent chance of making a difference when they behave trustingly, reach each student, read situations, create attractive invitations and ensure their delivery, and show willingness to negotiate. Even doing all of these things will not guarantee that an invitation will be accepted. The only sure way to avoid rejection is not to send invitations. But who wants to be a disinviting teacher in a disinviting school?

FOLLOWING THROUGH

After the educator's invitation is extended, received, and acknowledged, it can then be accepted, rejected, negotiated, or put on hold by others. But the process does not end there; the interaction concludes on the educator's side of the net. The final moves are made by the educator, who takes responsibility for following through on accepted invitations, analyzing and renegotiating unaccepted ones, and adding fresh ones.

An invitation provides a way of coming together for some worthwhile purpose. Following through begins with the teacher's reflection: Were they with me? Were we able to come together, even for a brief time, in mutually beneficial ways? If the teacher answers yes, the feeling should be a peak educative experience—one of those moments that make teaching so exciting. These moments are to be savored and then stored away, to be brought out later when you are feeling a bit low about teaching.

On the other hand, if the inviting transaction was less than successful, the teacher can examine what happened: Was the invitation unclear or inappropriate? Did the student need more time to consider? Did the invitation require too great a commitment of time or energy? Does the student lack the skills to be successful? Were there other factors that made the invitation unacceptable? Reflecting on what happened is an important way to increase the probability of future success. Schools that seek to be inviting set up ways that teachers can practice and discuss the strategies they are using.

To Send or Not to Send

The craft of inviting involves not only knowing *how* to invite, but also choosing *when* to invite. Inviting is an uncertain and risky business. Consider the choices and risks embedded in sending or not sending, accepting, or not accepting, invitations.

> Over 30 years ago, when I was a young girl, I attended a square dance. While there I spied a handsome young man standing alone. After watching him for a while, I summoned my courage, walked over to him and said: "Excuse me sir, do you dance?" He replied "No, I don't know how." And I said: "I'll teach you!" We've been dancing together ever since . . . during our 30 years of marriage.
>
> —A graduate student,
> The University of North Carolina at Greensboro

An invitation is an idea someone had, a choice someone made, and a risk someone took. Inviting others involves risks: risk of rejection; risk of being misunderstood or misinterpreted; risk of being accepted, but having things not work out as anticipated. Each of these risks can be minimized, but because human beings live in a less than totally certain world, risks will always be present. Would the human spirit want it otherwise? The greatest hazards in life are to risk nothing, send nothing, accept nothing, be nothing.

Although people take risks when they invite, there are greater risks in not inviting. Teachers who do not invite may be safe from rejection, misunderstanding, or involvement, but that is not what teachers should be. Students learn that they are able, valuable, and responsible when someone takes the risk of inviting them to feel that way.

In the inviting process, good intentions are necessary, but not sufficient. To be personally and professionally inviting, it is important to ask yourself: Is this the most appropriate and caring action I can take with this person at this time?

Choosing to behave in an inviting manner does not mean constantly sending affirming messages. Sometimes the most inviting thing one can do is *not* to send an invitation. For example, inviting a colleague to have a milk-shake when you know they are trying to lose weight is at best thoughtless, at worst, cruel. An ill-timed, inappropriate, or thoughtless invitation is often perceived as very disinviting. Offering a banner to "the best-behaved class" would be appealing to primary-school children, but the same offer made in a junior high school might be received with horror!

In considering the risks involved in inviting or not inviting, there are two general guidelines. The first is to *listen* and be sensitive to what might be perceived as appropriate and caring behavior. Second, when the evidence seems about equally divided between sending or not sending—send! If people invite, others may accept; if people don't, others can't. The choice to send can make the difference of a lifetime. Older adults, when looking back over their lives, report that they worry more about the things they did *not* do, rather than the things they did. Humans have a finite amount of time for inviting . . . an eternity for not doing so.

To Accept or Not to Accept

The inviting process is an interactive and interdependent activity that involves alternating between sending and accepting. Just as there are risks in sending and not sending, so too are there risks in accepting and not accepting.

Accepting an invitation is another way of saying "I trust you." This trust involves a special risk of vulnerability. Individuals don't have control over other people's trustworthiness, yet by accepting invitations they are placing themselves in the care of others. Ultimately, however, if individuals always choose control over risk, they run the even greater hazard described by Edgar Lee Masters in *Spoon River Anthology* (1922): "For love was offered me and I shrank from its disillusionment; sorrow knocked at my door, but I was afraid; ambition called to me, but I dreaded the chances. Yet all the while I hungered for meaning in my life" (p. 65). He continues by stating, "And now I know that we must lift the sail and catch the winds of destiny wherever they drive the boat" (p. 65). When chances of success are good, Masters seems to say, take the chance.

> Accepting an invitation is another way of saying "I trust you." This trust involves a special risk of vulnerability.

A guideline for accepting life's opportunities is a willingness to risk. The risk of living in a world where people avoid involvement seems greater than the risk of being hurt. There are reasons, of course, why certain invitations cannot or should not be accepted. A reasonable rule of thumb seems to be the following: Accept those invitations worth accepting and decline the rest graciously. Even the process of not accepting an invitation can be done in an inviting manner.

Understanding the dynamics of sending/not sending, accepting/not accepting has just begun. But in simple terms, it seems to go something like this:

If I don't invite, you can't accept.
If you can't accept, you won't invite.
If you don't invite, I can't accept.
If there are no invitations, there is no development.

The central ingredient in understanding the craft of inviting is the intentional desire to be a beneficial presence in the lives of fellow human beings. Without the desire, the theory and practice of Invitational Education is meaningless. Students can benefit from the inviting process the way flowers benefit from sunshine. Teaching is a delicate and fragile humane art, intentionally built upon care, optimism, respect, and trust. The purposeful craft of inviting is anchored in these qualities.

SUMMARY

This chapter presented the idea that life in schools, including security and success, depends in large part on the intentionally developed skills of educators. It has introduced the idea that the craft of inviting requires commitment, sensitivity, courage, and imagination. Inviting, at times, can be a complex and elusive process of decoding messages, reaching for meanings, making connections, and recognizing subtle nuances of human interaction. This is no easy task. The craft of inviting is more a journey than a destination, however. No one reaches his or her full potential, yet development is possible and growth can be enjoyable. The next chapter will take the craft of inviting into some of the most challenging issues educators face.

FURTHER REFLECTIONS AND ACTIVITIES

1. Think of an issue in your school related to an existing policy, program, or process for which the response to alternatives has been "This is how things have always been done," or "Nothing can be done about this." Discuss the improvements needed and what might be needed to get there. Consider what stakeholders in the school and community can contribute.
2. The "Doing With" section of this chapter includes seven skills for developing an educator's invitational skills. Think of a student who has presented academic or behavioral challenges in your class or school. How might these "doing with" skills change your approach, build trust, and encourage the student to choose more beneficial behaviors?

3. Reflect on a time when you did not accept a well-intended invitation from someone. Consider what caused you to avoid accepting? What risk might you have perceived? What benefits might you have enjoyed had you accepted?
4. Activity for Faculty Meeting:

Human Graph
Based on an exercise designed by colleague Judy Lehr Guarino

Post four signs with one of the following labels in different corners of the meeting room:

- Intentionally Disinviting
- Unintentionally Disinviting
- Unintentionally Inviting
- Intentionally Inviting

Read one of the scenarios below. Then ask participants to stand in front of the sign that best describes how they would label the level of function for the person's action. Then ask the suggested questions. Participants may move if something a colleague says causes them to change their perception of the situation.

Scenario 1

Mr. Brown teaches 7th-grade math. He gives the students a worksheet to complete at their desks. He notices that Sheila has her head down and appears to be asleep. He approaches her desk, taps her on the shoulder, and says, "I'd really like to see you practice this skill." She ignores his request and turns her head away from him, where upon he says, "Sheila, get busy." She doesn't respond. He then writes a behavior referral and sends her to the office.

- At what level was Mr. Brown functioning?
- Why did you select that level of functioning?
- How would you have handled the situation?

Scenario 2

Ms. West, a popular high school social studies teacher, sees Ashley, one of her students in the cafeteria. Ashley was absent from Ms. West's 1st-period class that morning. She has also missed 4 days of 1st period over the last 2 weeks. Yet Ms. West has seen her on campus. Ms. West approaches Ashley at the table where she is seated with other students and says, jokingly, "So you got to sleep late this morning, huh?" Ashley responds, "You didn't really see me today, OK?" She winks at Ms. West and starts to walk out of the room.

- At what level was Ms. West functioning?
- Why did you select that level of functioning?

- How could the teacher have helped the student to take responsibility for her classwork and behavior?

Scenario 3

Mrs. Mahoney, the school counselor, is conducting a support group for children whose parents are going through a divorce. This group meets once a week, during Mr. Greco's social studies class. He was disturbed because two of his students were missing a whole class every week. One day, he approached Mrs. Mahoney and asked if his students can just go every other week.

Mrs. Mahoney told him that at this point in the students' lives, it was more important to be in the support group. Mr. Greco expressed concern about the students and asked if there was anything he needed to know in order to help his students. Mrs. Mahoney responded, "You know I cannot violate confidentiality."

- At what level was Mrs. Mahoney functioning?
- At what level was Mr. Greco functioning?

Scenario 4

Ms. Franklin is a 4th-grade classroom teacher. She has worked in the school for 24 years. Scott is in her class this year, and Scott's brother, Eddie, was in her class 2 years prior. Eddie was always very forgetful and unprepared for class. Ms. Franklin often calls Scott "Eddie" by mistake. One day after referring to Scott as "Eddie," she apologizes by saying, "Sorry Scott, you just remind me so much of your brother."

- At what level was Ms. Franklin functioning?
- Why did you choose that level?
- If you were Ms. Franklin, what would you have said?

Scenario 5

Jenny Ward Is in her third year of college, studying to be a math teacher. She has had the same math professor for several teaching pedagogy classes. One day, after Jenny struggled in presenting a minilesson to her peers, the professor spoke to her privately after class and started the conversation by saying, "I know math comes really easily to you, Jenny, but I don't think you are cut out to be a teacher of math. Perhaps you might want to consider changing your major. There are lots of careers in which your math skills will serve you well."

- At what level was the professor operating?
- How would you have started the conversation?

CHAPTER 5

Inviting in the Rain

Neighborhood gangs and their initiations, receiving upwards of one hundred unaccompanied minors, students living in poverty and various other traumas are just a few of the challenges our middle school staff faces each year. Invitational Education has become our rock. Optimism has become the norm and resonates throughout our administration, skilled staff, and young scholars. Instead of standing at my door with concerns and problems, my faculty problem-solve with conviction and, more often than not, creates success stories. We now have a deeper understanding of what drives students' choices of behavior and how influential our words, tone, and actions can be. Our school is not just surviving today's challenges, it is embracing them and meeting them head on.

—Dr. Tracy Hudson, Charles Mulligan Middle School, Central Islip, NY
personal correspondence, February 26, 2018

Chapter 5 is titled "Inviting in the Rain" because we recognize that it is not easy to be inviting when "the sun isn't shining" and things aren't going the way one wants. As difficult as it is to act dependably and intentionally with respect, trust, optimism, and care, these qualities are exactly what is required to successfully manage the most challenging situations that occur in your school. Students who challenge inviting practices the most can also benefit the most.

INVITATIONAL EDUCATION IN A VIOLENT SOCIETY

Perhaps never before has there been such concern and need for students to have a safe school environment. Many educators have on-the-scene knowledge of serious confrontations, fights, suicides, killings, and countless other traumatic experiences. They have experienced trauma right along with their students. Teachers have also suffered verbal abuse, physical assault, and even death in dealing with students, parents, and community members. Following another horrific school shooting on February 14, 2018, at Marjory Stoneman Douglas High School in Florida, 19 leading experts in the study of school violence (Astor et al., 2018) authored an eight-point

"Call for Action to Prevent Gun Violence in the United States of America."
Two of the eight identified needs speak directly to the importance of positive
school climate. These are key components of Invitational Education.

- A national requirement for all schools to assess school climate and
  maintain physically and emotionally safe conditions and positive
  school environments that protect all students and adults from
  bullying, discrimination, harassment, and assault, and
- Reform of school discipline to reduce exclusionary practices and
  foster positive social, behavioral, emotional, and academic success
  for students. (p. 2)

The importance and influence of positive school climate has long been
marginalized, while the pressure of high-stakes testing consumed educators'
time and resources. How tragic that it took the loss of so many lives to
balance educational priorities and focus finally on the social and emotional
health of our schools.

A Hostage Situation

A major misunderstanding of Invitational Education is that the inviting approach is fine when the sun is shining and everything is going well, but it
won't work when facing dangerous situations. In fact, the reverse is true.
The inviting approach is at its best in trying—even life-threatening—situations. One such experience happened to friend and colleague Jim Ratledge,
principal of the Montvale School, a K–8 school in Blount County, Tennessee
(Mansfield, 1999). The school has about 850 students. Here is how Jim
described this critical incident:

> At the end of fifth period on a typical day, a teacher brought two
> students to tell me that they wanted to "tell" me something. Little did
> I know that this was the beginning of an educator's worst nightmare!
> A student had brought a gun to school and had it in his waistband.

Jim went to the student's classroom and asked the student to accom-
pany him to the principal's office. He informed the student of the charge
and that he would have to be searched. There was no gun in his waistband.
However, as Jim and the student talked, the student suddenly reached in the
crotch area of his pants and said, "Mr. Ratledge, I really hate to do this."
He produced an automatic .380 Beretta with a full clip in the handgun and
pointed it at Jim.

For the next 4 hours Jim was a hostage. During that time Jim quietly
talked with the student in a respectful manner. They talked about everything
from the Bible to Babylon. Jim was able to keep the student calm. When the

student said he had messed up and ruined his life, Jim assured him that he was a bright young man with a wonderful future. After 4 hours, the student gave Jim the gun and the critical incident ended.

Throughout the ordeal Jim practiced the basics of Invitational Education: Showing respect for the student, remaining optimistic about outcomes, building a trusting relationship, and intentionally working to redirect the student's perceptions. Here are a few basic rules that Jim followed in defusing the situation:

1. Jim did not demean or patronize the student.
2. Jim calmed the student down by his choice of behavior.
3. Jim did not threaten or try to touch or grab the student.
4. Jim worked on finding a solution to the situation.
5. Jim worked to enter the perceptual world of the hurting student.
6. Jim allowed the student to fully express his feelings without interruption. Once the student reached the top of "emotion mountain," he had fully expressed himself, the tensions were diminished, and he was then able to consider alternate behaviors.

Jim's inviting approach is well supported by today's brain research. Dan Siegel (2007), codirector of the UCLA Mindful Awareness Research Center, explains that when we experience strong emotions, the limbic part of the brain (responsible for fight, flight, or freeze responses) takes over, and the prefrontal cortex (responsible for decisionmaking, empathy, and higher-order skills) disengages, causing us not to be able to consider alternative ways of addressing our feelings and needs. Jim allowed the student to be present with his emotions until they subsided and the student was then able to access the thinking part of his brain. Generating voluntary compliance not only supports how the brain functions—it is truly the hallmark of professionalism.

Costs of Violence

To combat the problem of school violence and promote school safety, educators and the larger community have often relied on traditional law enforcement methods. Such methods include placing metal detectors at school entrances, posting warning signs, hiring security guards to patrol hallways and school grounds, building security fences, mounting surveillance cameras, outlawing book bags, and conducting unannounced pat-down searches of students and their lockers. These methods, although now required by law in many places, are better suited for prisons and detention centers.

Law enforcement methods rely heavily on surveillance, penalties, and punishments. These measures detract significantly from human dignity and worth. In the school, such methods include student suspensions, expulsions, alternative school placement for offenders, arrests by law enforcement officials, felony charges, and various penalties and fines placed on parents or guardians.

Although sometimes effective and probably needed, traditional law enforcement methods applied to schools carry major negative side effects. These include possible violations of students' civil rights; sharply reduced instruction time during the school day; a decline in morale of teachers, students, and parents; and a financial burden on meager educational dollars. Let's consider these negative side effects.

> *Although sometimes effective and probably needed, traditional law enforcement methods applied to schools carry major negative side effects.*

- **Civil Rights Costs:** A democratic society is the result of efforts, often at great personal expense, to ensure the civil rights of all its citizens. These valued rights were not easily obtained, but can be easily eroded, especially by those whose mindset is to fight fire with fire. In fact, often a better way to fight fire is with water. Denying students' basic civil rights in the name of law and order works against the democratic ethos that schools are supposed to promote and sends the message that schools are primarily about control. In their research on motivation, Deci and Ryan (2017) demonstrate that while control-oriented approaches may cause someone to become compliant, they also lead to alienation and defiance.
- **Educational Costs:** Time on task is a major variable in student learning. Students typically arrive just minutes before their first class. Furthermore, school buses commonly arrive within moments of one another. The result creates a frenzy of activity. Even without the process of screening with metal detectors, human logjams are common at the major entrances of many schools. The time taken each morning to adequately move individual students and their materials through a school metal detector detracts heavily from the length of time devoted to the teaching/learning process. The same is true of locker checks and pat-down searches. Such activities weaken the school academically.
- **Morale Costs:** When students are treated as potential threats, they are likely to behave accordingly. Metal detectors, security guards, and police officers (whose main job in some schools is catching students doing something against school rules), surveillance cameras, locker checks, and body searches create a pervasive atmosphere of distrust and apprehension among faculty, staff, students, and parents. Such negative feelings within the school undoubtedly affect morale and the teaching/learning process.

- *Financial Costs:* Although it is difficult to obtain accurate figures, it seems logical that the cost of purchasing metal detectors, hiring more security guards, and adding other security measures takes away from resources designed to promote student learning. A single walk-through metal detector costs approximately $6,000, and each detector is typically staffed by two to four security officers. Such staffing, in addition to metal detector maintenance charges, adds to the cost of operation and takes away teaching dollars.

When compared with such powerful-sounding approaches to the educative process as *assertive* discipline, *tough* love, and teacher *empowerment*, Invitational Education may sound weak and ill-equipped to confront the major problems of education. The reverse is true. Inviting behavior is strong; dictating behavior is weak. Educators who rely on dictating and controlling may find themselves in difficult straits when confronted by students who also have formidable power. Time-out corners, in-school suspensions, corporal punishment, or expulsion are unlikely to impress students who face the harsh realities of grinding poverty, gang warfare, drive-by killings, or bitter inequalities. It is useful to remember that no one in the school is without power. How that power is used is determined by how the person sees the world at the moment of action.

Adults often misinterpret the cause of some adolescent behavior. Based on changes in the fundamental circuits of the teenage brain, Dan Siegel (2014) identifies four qualities of adolescent minds that are worth consideration: novelty seeking, social engagement, increased emotional intensity, and creative exploration. All four characteristics contribute to a teenager choosing dangerous behaviors for the thrill of it, with little consideration for the consequences. In addition, their drive for social connection in peer groups increases the isolation of teens from adults, as does their tendency to reject adults and adult knowledge. This underscores the need for positive communication and interaction with adults—instead of isolating teens through school suspensions—at the time when adult relationships and guidance are needed most.

Haberman (1994) presents a compelling case for gentle teaching as an antidote for a violent society. He maintains that educators have no choice other than gentle teaching when working with at-risk students. He wrote, "Beyond kindergarten and the first two grades, teachers can no longer physically control their students with external sanctions or fear. For teachers to pretend that they have means which can force students to learn or even comply is a dangerous myth which can make poverty schools as coercive and violent as the neighborhood outside the school" (p. 4). Relying on coercion and force demonstrates little regard for viable alternatives or respect for students; it lacks educational character, intelligence, or imagination. This chapter will first address moderate and typical discipline processes, and then move to more serious concerns.

AN INVITATIONAL APPROACH TO GOOD DISCIPLINE

Maintaining good discipline in schools has been, and probably always will be, a major concern of educators. Students tend to resist external control because it restricts personal choice and limits freedom. This love of freedom is a valuable part of the democratic ethic and should be cultivated rather than condemned. At the same time, teachers are responsible for maintaining reasonable control in the classroom and for achieving the goals set forth by society. To maintain order (usually called discipline), teachers have tried just about everything.

Earlier methods of discipline were essentially negative, with fear and punishment playing major roles. One of the first schoolhouses built in the United States had a whipping post (Manning, 1959) and in the "good old days" many painful techniques were devised to inflict physical punishment on erring students. Fear played a major role in maintaining discipline, and children received ominous warnings from home, school, and pulpit that, as James Whitcomb Riley said in *Little Orphant Annie,* "the gobble-uns'll git you ef you don't watch out!" (1916, p. 1170).

Fortunately, more modern methods of maintaining classroom discipline are generally positive. Many researchers and writers (Brady et al., 2015; Wood & Freeman-Loftis, 2015) and others have provided practical tips on how to deal in a respectful and caring manner with student misconduct. Behavior modification techniques that seek to reinforce desirable behavior and extinguish undesirable behavior are often effective. For behavior modification to work, the classroom is usually arranged so that when students behave in desirable ways, desirable things happen to them. Reinforcement of this sort relies primarily on rewards rather than punishments to modify and shape student behavior.

As Invitational Education is based on the concept that there is only one kind of motivation, it seems prudent to pause to provide some caution with regard to the use of rewards (or punishments) to influence someone's choice of behavior. Deci and Ryan's more than 40 years of research on self-determination theory (Deci, 1971, 1985, 1995; Deci & Ryan, 1987, 1991, 2008, 2017), provide strong support for an inviting approach to discipline. They label rewards and punishments as "extrinsic controls" rather than the more commonly used term "extrinsic motivators." They counsel us to be mindful of our intention when using rewards, and suggest using rewards to *acknowledge* an accomplishment, rather than to *get* someone to do something. It is also interesting to note that controls "have clearly detrimental effects on the performance of any tasks that require creativity, conceptual understanding, or flexible problem solving" (Deci, 1995, p. 51). Offering people extrinsic rewards actually causes productivity and creativity to decrease. One reason is that we all have a limited amount of attention we can direct to a task. When part of our attention becomes focused on the reward, it leaves us with less attention available to address the task at hand.

Deci and Ryan's many experiments also demonstrated that when prompted to do something in order to receive a reward, people often stop the desirable behavior when the reward is no longer available. In alignment with Invitational Education, they suggest that educators not try to control or motivate students, but instead focus on creating three conditions in which students' desire to learn can flourish: opportunities for choice, competence, and relatedness. Their work underscores the foundations of Invitational Education as well as the unintended consequences that may occur when choosing a particular behavioral technique.

While many contemporary behavioral approaches treat discipline primarily as a matter of employing certain punishment and reward techniques, Invitational Education focuses on the larger issues of teacher perception, stance, and action. As an inviting teacher, one strives to develop a fair-minded perspective and works to maintain good discipline through caring and consistent expectations for oneself and for others.

An inviting approach to discipline centers on the dignity of people. Whether intentionally or unintentionally, educators sometimes run rough-shod over the personal feelings of students. "My last name is Turley," a student wrote, "and my science teacher always called me 'Turkey' and laughed. At first, I felt hurt, and now I'm just resentful." When educators em-

> *An inviting approach to discipline centers on the dignity of people.*

ploy tasteless humor, ridicule, and lack of respect for students, it is not surprising that students and their families reply in kind. In practical terms this means that teachers should consistently practice common courtesy and civility and encourage these practices in others. A colleague, Robert "Buzz" Lee, believes this process is so important that he signs a "no-cut contract" with each of his students at the beginning of each semester. This contract stipulates that "I won't disinvite myself, I won't disinvite you. I will invite myself, I will invite you." Everyone is encouraged to sign the contract.

Students who are consistently treated with dignity, care, and respect are less likely to cause problems in the classroom. Wonderful things can happen when students sense they are respected, are seen as responsible, and have their feelings considered. Conversely, students who think that teachers are out to embarrass them, and that the system is geared to convince them that they are worthless, unable, and irresponsible, will find ways to rebel, disrupt, and seek revenge—as humans have always done to voice their discontent and resentment. This is powerfully illustrated by the words of Shakespeare's hunchback, Richard: "And therefore, since I cannot prove a lover, to entertain these fair well-spoken days, I am determined to prove a villain, and hate the idle pleasures of these days" (*Richard III,* 1.1.28–31). Some students reason that, "if I can't be the best, I'll be the best at being the worst." When students feel disinvited in school, they are likely to respond in kind.

Beyond manifesting respect for students, good discipline is developed and maintained by teachers who believe that teaching should be as interesting and involving as possible, and students should experience honest academic success. When teachers recognize boredom and lack of success as causal agents in misbehavior, they are more likely to seek ways to make their teaching as engaging, exciting, and successful as possible. Everyday discipline problems tend to diminish when students are interested, involved, and succeeding in school.

Finally, the ability to invite good discipline depends on the teacher's perception about what constitutes misbehavior. These beliefs vary considerably from teacher to teacher, school to school, and decade to decade. In 1848, for example, a North Carolina high school listed as misbehaviors boys and girls playing together, girls wearing long fingernails, and boys neglecting to bow before going home! Today, most educators agree that rules should be reasonable, enforceable, and educationally relevant.

A growing problem in many schools is major punishment for minor infractions, such as not showing respect for teachers. Too often in the past, educators attempted to enforce rules that were authoritarian, clearly disinviting, and—like regulations pertaining to hairstyles, clothing, and jewelry—had little relevance to education. An example of the irrelevance of some control efforts was encountered by one of the authors. A high school girl was suspended from school because she had dyed her hair a bright blue. The thought flashed through the author's mind that if the principal suspended everyone with dyed hair, there might not be a teacher left. With fewer, more reasonable rules, fewer rules will be broken.

By now the reader may be thinking, "I believe all these things about discipline, but some students still insist on being disruptive." This belief has been around for a long time and certainly has a ring of truth to it. Some students resist any form of control, and concerns about behavior will continue to exist even in the most inviting school environment.

When misbehavior exceeds reasonable limits, educators should ask themselves: "What is happening here? Is the student upset or ill? Is there some challenging situation happening outside of school? Is the student experiencing strong negative emotions and needing strategies for managing those feelings? Are certain factors in the school, such as temperature, class size, time of day, or behavior by others eliciting misbehavior? How does this student view themselves and others in the school? Does the misbehaving student need professional counseling or psychological help? Has this student been able to enjoy honest success experiences in school?" This is also the time for the teacher to consider the reasons for their own actions: "Am I concerned about this because of my own insecurities, biases, or prejudices? Have I triggered the misbehavior by employing ridicule or sarcasm, relying on the grade book to maintain discipline, or by screaming, yelling, or haranguing?" When satisfactory and fair-minded answers to questions like these do not excuse or explain the misbehavior, an appropriate consequence is necessary. But even at this point, what educators believe about penalties makes a difference.

If educators believe that penalties should be humane and used sparingly, they will use temporary denial of student privileges rather than public humiliation (writing names on the board), corporal punishment, exclusion from school, or psychological warfare. Punishment should not give students the resentful feeling of being wronged. The object of a penalty is to encourage the student to reflect on the offense, recognize why it was inappropriate, and take appropriate steps to correct it.

MANAGING CONFLICT: RULE OF THE 6 Cs

Educators, like everyone else in society, face vexing conflicts and pressurized situations. Practitioners of Invitational Education seek to handle these challenges in the most decent, respectful, and caring ways possible. This section on managing conflict and defusing difficult situations is based on a book written by two of the three authors and a talented colleague, Jack Schmidt. For a more in-depth understanding of "Rule of the 6 Cs," visit *From Conflict to Conciliation: How to Defuse Difficult Situations* (Purkey, Schmidt, & Novak, 2010.) The rule is to employ the lowest C first and to move upward through higher Cs only as necessary. The 6 Cs are concern, confer, consult, confront, combat, and conciliation.

Using this approach, concerns are resolved in a principled, effective manner. These concerns may be as minor as a student chewing gum in class or as major as stealing, lying, or confronting the teacher or physically abusing other students. Will the invitational approach work in all situations? Of course not. However, it will give the educator a position from which to operate and a valuable guide for addressing difficult situations.

Anyone can escalate a conflict or aggravate a problem.

Whether minor or major, personal or professional, real or imagined, Invitational Education provides a practical way to resolve the concern at the lowest possible level, with the least amount of time and energy, with the minimal possible costs, and most important, in the most humane and respectful manner possible.

Anyone can escalate a conflict or aggravate a problem. It takes trust, respect, optimism, and intentionality to resolve the conflict at the lowest possible C, beginning with concern.

Concern

In any situation that involves real or potential conflict, the educator who employs Invitational Education first reflects on questions such as these:

- Is this situation really a matter of concern?
- Can it be safely and wisely overlooked without undue personal stress?
- Will this resolve itself without my intervention?
- Does this involve a matter of ethics, morality, or legality?
- Is this the best time for me to be concerned about or address this?
- Is this an actionable concern?
- Are sufficient resources available for me to address this?
- Can this be reconceptualized as a "situation," or, better yet, as an "opportunity"?
- Am I concerned because of my own prejudices, biases, or need to impress people?
- Have I conducted a perception check with a trusted colleague to validate my own interpretation of a situation?
- Is this just one of the inevitable tensions and opportunities involved in living in a contemporary, pluralistic democracy?

Real or imagined concerns in school can often be handled at this lowest level by asking and answering the above questions. The potential conflict may quickly resolve itself.

There are times, of course, when a concern is sufficiently troublesome that it requires action. Then it is time to confer.

Confer

To confer is to initiate an informal and private conversation with another person. The individual who embraces Invitational Education begins by signaling the desire for a positive and nonthreatening interaction (using the person's name, friendly eye contact, nonaggressive posture, smile, handshake, and so forth). Then the individual briefly explains, in an intentionally nonconfrontational and respectful way, what the concern is, why it is a concern, and what is proposed to resolve it. For example: "Bill, when you come late to class, I spend extra time looking at your admission slip. Please come on time tomorrow. *Would you do this for me?*" Asking for what is wanted is vital. Although the reader may think that the student should do it for his or her own benefit, it is the teacher's concern that is being addressed. The purpose of the 6 Cs is to help manage the teacher's concern "This tardiness is bugging me!" Obtaining commitment by asking, "Will you do this for me?" is very important and connects with what follows.

At the conferring level, consider these questions:

- After expressing my concern, have I carefully listened to encourage honest communication?
- Is there a clear understanding by both parties regarding the nature of the concern?
- Do both parties know *why* the situation is a concern?
- Is there room for compromise or reconceptualization? (Perhaps the student is late for class because the bus was running late. This may require action regarding bus schedules.)
- Have I clearly asked for what I want? ("Will you do this for me?") Again, it is important to obtain commitment.
- Is my concern important enough to move to a higher level?

In most situations, a one-on-one, respectful, and informal conference, *always in private*, will resolve the concern. However, it is useful to record and document the concern for possible future use. In cases where conferring does not solve the problem, consulting is appropriate.

Consult

Consultation is more formal than conferring. Consultation involves clear and direct talk about a concern that has already been discussed and not yet resolved. For example, "Bill, last week you told me that you would get to school on time, but this morning you were late again. I expect you to keep your word." Questions to be considered at the consultation stage include these:

- Again, is it clear to both parties what is expected?
- Are there ways that I can assist the student in abiding by previous decisions? (A morning wake-up call for a few days might work miracles.)
- Have the consequences of not resolving the situation at this early stage been considered? (Don't wait too long to express valid concerns.)
- Will confrontation resolve the situation? (Is it worth the effort?)

Should consultation, after repeated attempts, not work, then it is time for confrontation.

Confront

Confrontation is a no-nonsense effort to resolve the concern. At this time, it is important again to explain in detail why the situation is a concern. Now is the time to be direct and frank and to explain why the situation continues to be a concern. Point out that this situation has been addressed previously and repeatedly, and that progress has been insufficient.

It is appropriate and caring at this level to speak of consequences. For example, "Bill, if you continue to come late to class, I will put you on report. I don't want to do this. Would you please come to class on time for me?" Now is the time to move to logical consequences of behavior. Questions to ask at this serious level include these:

- Have I made a sincere effort to manage this concern at each of the lower levels?
- Do I have documented evidence that I have made efforts to resolve the conflict at lower levels?
- Do I have sufficient authority, power, and will to go through with stated consequences?

When the first four levels have been applied in turn, each party is likely to know that the stated consequences are fair and impartial. Should the conflict persist in spite of the first four Cs, then the fifth C level is appropriate.

Combat

At this ultimate level, the word "combat" is used as a verb rather than a noun. The purpose is to combat the situation, not the person. The word "combat" stresses the seriousness of the concern. It also indicates that because the concern has not been resolved at lower levels, this is the time to move to consequences. This requires direct, immediate, and firm action.

At this ultimate level, the word "combat" is used as a verb rather than a noun. The purpose is to combat the situation, not the person.

Sometimes educators are forced to bypass lower levels and go directly to combat—for example, when one student is physically abusing another. But even here, Invitational Education warns against unnecessary force. A valuable resource for educators is to become acquainted with crisis situations and how to respond to them. Many schools provide this training for faculty and staff.

For obvious reasons, combat situations are to be avoided whenever and wherever possible. At the combat level, stakes are high, and there are likely to be winners and losers. Who wins and who loses is often unpredictable. Moreover, having combat situations requires a great deal of energy that could be better spent in teaching and learning. Yet, when lower Cs have not resolved the concern, it is time to enter the arena. Wherever possible, try not to "take the hill without covering fire": Try to ensure that previous steps have been taken. In preparing for the combat level, consider the following:

- Do I have clear documentation that other avenues were sought?
- Even at this late date, is there a way to find avenues of compromise?
- Is there sufficient support and resources to successfully combat the situation?

After each level, but especially after the combat level, it is important to take time to be reflective and work toward conciliation.

Conciliation

To conciliate means to bring together, to unite after a period of separation. Although this is especially important if the combat stage has been reached, it is also necessary after each of the other four levels to restore a working stability and openness to new possibilities.

Combating a situation, no matter how well intended and thoughtful the efforts, can still leave a feeling of uncertainty, uneasiness, or discomfort. Especially after the combat level, it is beneficial to spend time reflecting on questions like these:

- Did I let the fire die down and not act hot-headed?
- Did I give people time and space to resettle?
- Did I use intermediaries to help restore a positive relationship?
- Did I trust the process and act with a quiet confidence?
- Am I willing to see the situation in a new light and make amends?

In each of the five previous levels, there is an increase in intensity and a focus on isolating the point of contention. Conciliation, on the other hand, requires a decrease in intensity as you take a step back from a situation to reconstruct a deeper and more meaningful unity. It becomes a time to learn important things about yourself and live more insightfully as a result of dealing with conflicting situations.

Regardless of the level at which the concern is resolved, the educator who employs Invitational Education consistently maintains respect, trust, optimism, care, and intentionality throughout the entire process.

Regardless of the level at which the concern is resolved, the educator who employs Invitational Education consistently maintains respect, trust, optimism, care, and intentionality throughout the entire process.

By handling concerns at the lowest possible level, educators who employ Invitational Education save energy, reduce hostility, and avoid acrimony. By applying the 6 Cs, it is possible, even in the most difficult situations, to manage conflicts. This is a major strength of Invitational Education: Invitational Education can be used to understand and develop strategies for dealing with concerns, up to and including violence in schools.

UNDERSTANDING VIOLENCE

Haberman (1994) has identified at least five factors that set the stage for violence. Although his research was conducted more than 2 decades ago, his findings seem valid in today's world.

1. *Lack of trust in adults.* A general breakdown in adult reliability, intentionality, competence, and truthfulness has caused many young people to withdraw from adults and become suspicious of their motives.
2. *Presence of violence.* According to the National Survey of Children's Exposure to Violence (Turner et al., 2009), 60% of urban youth reported experiencing or witnessing violence in the past year. This violence is magnified by mass media that fixate on murder and mayhem.
3. *Lack of hope.* Countless young people simply see no hope for themselves. They view themselves as without options and as going nowhere, particularly in school.
4. *The presence of mindless bureaucracy.* The system treats teachers and students as functionaries and continually evaluates according to conformity and performance, rather than creativity and effort.
5. *The influence of a culture of authoritarianism.* The use of power and coercion as the perceived way to handle situations is often supported by politicians, press, and public.

Invitational Education directly counteracts each of these triggering factors for school violence. Although there are other reasons why violence exists in schools, these five suggest how factors work together to encourage frustration and elicit aggression in students.

The following suggestions are representative of how Invitational Education can help to promote safety and reduce violence in schools.

CREATING AND MAINTAINING SAFE SCHOOLS

Inviting schools are safe schools where students feel valued and connected to their school and community. The Prevention Institute (n.d.; https://www.preventioninstitute.org) describes characteristics of effective school-based violence-prevention programs:

- A strong commitment to reaching all students and staff with the message that violence, harassment, and intolerance are unacceptable in the school environment.
- Involving all students, staff, parents, and interested community members in learning about violence and how to prevent it.
- Eliminating barriers to communication among groups of students.
- Involving students as critical and valued partners in violence prevention initiatives.
- Collaborating closely and effectively with community, media, and policing agencies.

Here are 21 examples of initiatives, resources, and simple tips that inviting schools can consider to promote school safety and reduce violence:

1. **Create service learning experiences for students.** In addition to athletic, arts, and club activities, young people thrive in service learning experiences where they identify a community or school need and lead a long-term project to make a difference in their world. Students who participate in meaningful service initiatives increase connections to their school and community, learn that they have the power to influence change, and are perceived more positively by their surrounding community.

2. **Organize peer mediation teams.** Helping students learn how to take responsibility and resolve arguments through peer mediation is beneficial. Students can suggest those fellow students they believe would be effective peer mediators for a specific school year. This team of peer mediators can then be trained to work together with fellow students to resolve differences. Students involved in conflicts can choose either staff interventions or a session with the peer mediation team.

3. **Organize peer mentoring.** Students helping students promotes an atmosphere of encouragement. Older students can help acculturate younger students to new buildings, new rules, and new behaviors. Older students can also help younger students with school projects and assignments. Such relationships are helpful in at least three ways. First, younger students receive individual attention and

encouragement. Second, it suggests that someone is interested in their progress. Third, older students are likely to learn that their actions as role models have a significant effect upon younger students.

4. *Organize adult mentoring.* Adult mentors are volunteer parents, staff, alumni, or community members who become a dependable adult in a student's life, serving as someone the student can trust and talk to. Adults who are trained in mentoring may also provide helpful assistance at large school activities.

5. *Look for causes.* Sometimes the causes of violence in schools lie with systems rather than people. For example, running in the halls, pushing, shoving, and fighting may be triggered by inadequate or inappropriate time periods for lunch, change of class, or bus departure. Changing policies may reduce or eliminate some causes of violence.

6. *Stamp out rumors immediately.* Rumors have the potential to ignite violent reactions. The best way to combat rumors is to continuously provide immediate and accurate information. Rumors spring up when reliable information is lacking. School websites, email, social media, and automated telephone calls can all be used to provide accurate and up-to-date information that helps stamp out rumors.

7. *Respond promptly to incidents of bullying, harassment, and discrimination.* Develop and share your procedures for reporting and responding to acts of bullying, harassment, and discrimination. This includes student-to-student, adult-to-adult, and student-to-adult incidents. Staff, students, parents, and community members should know how to report incidents, and all staff members in the school need to know their responsibility for reporting incidents to school administration. As defined by Juhnke et al., in *School Bullying and Violence* (2020), the three main bullying categories are verbal, social, and physical bullying. Students and staff members should be trained to recognize incidents and understand the difference between bullying and a conflict. A designated school administrator should keep a written log of incidents reported and what was done in response to them. This provides documentation of patterns of negative behavior by anyone in and around the school. Find positive ways to support, respect, and guide all students involved.

8. *Organize a crisis team.* Most school counselors have the professional experience and training to organize, train, and direct teams of students, parents, faculty, and staff in crisis management. Inevitably, emergency events occur. These crises may be natural (weather,

fire, flood, and so forth) or societal (an armed intruder, a suicide, a student riot, and so on). It is essential that the school have a well-planned, quick-response crisis team in position to provide the necessary emotional support and guidance for students, their families, and faculty and staff. Some schools partner with neighboring districts in developing their crisis plans. They agree to share staff when an issue arises that requires many more mental health professionals than one school typically has on staff.

9. ***Teach social and emotional skills.*** There are many evidence-based programs that provide easy-to-lead activities for building community and developing self-awareness, self-management, social awareness, relationship, and decisionmaking skills that help all students (and staff) to become more skillful in how they communicate and respond to challenges and stresses in their lives. Over time, the social norms of the school will become more positive, making it easier for a student to choose positive behaviors. Opportunities to discuss issues and practice skills can significantly reduce negative behaviors, bullying, and discrimination. These activities can be led by any school adult in an advisory period, morning meeting, or, as part of the classroom teacher's lessons. Once presented, social–emotional skills can be infused into all aspects of the school curriculum.

10. ***Teach mindfulness practices to students and staff.*** In this fast-paced, demanding world, our minds are constantly filled with thoughts and strong emotions. Mindfulness practices help us to be fully present and avoid being hijacked by negative emotions that cause us to ruminate about the past or be anxious about the future. Mindfulness practices help us to be aware of our thoughts and emotions without feeling the need to immediately act on them. We become skillful at putting space between stimulus and our response, which provides us time to calm our emotions and fully access the prefrontal cortex—the part of the brain responsible for skills like decisionmaking, emotional balance, and empathy.

11. ***Introduce staff to Nonviolent Communication strategies.*** Marshall Rosenberg's foundational work, *Nonviolent Communication* (2015), provides a simple and effective four-part process to communicate empathically, through observation, feelings, needs, and requests. Known as NVC, this process develops skills in listening for and identifying the feelings and needs of others, as well as ourselves, without judgment or blame, then learning how to make requests that would enrich lives without demands. Resources available at The Center for Nonviolent Communication (NVC), https://www.cnvc.org

12. **Train staff in Collaborative & Proactive Solutions.** Too often, efforts to change challenging student behavior do not work, further alienate the student from staff, and reinforce a negative self-concept. Ross Greene's *Lost at School* (2014) introduces Collaborative & Proactive Solutions, which help teachers and parents to identify the problems and lagging skills causing the challenging behavior and use a simple process for acknowledging and identifying the child's feelings and needs, and then collaborating on a solution. Resources available at https://www.livesinthebalance.org

13. **Teach conflict management and restorative practices.** Everyone in the school, including faculty, staff, students, and volunteers, should receive comprehensive training in conflict management, crisis interventions, and restorative practices. Within an invitational framework, these like-minded strategies resolve conflicts in respectful and supportive ways, often replacing punishment with agreements to provide restitution and restore relationships. Parent and adult caregiver education programs that provide similar training for families can also be introduced at "parent university" meetings and in classes for adult caregivers. Resources available at International Institute for Restorative Practices, https://www.iirp.edu

14. **Reprimand in private.** People respond differently when they think others are observing their behavior. When students are to be corrected or disciplined, do this in private. This demonstrates respect for students and may defuse a dangerous situation. (This was stated in the section describing the 6 Cs, but is worth repeating here.)

15. **Be a cheerleader.** Provide consistent encouragement to students who are experiencing difficulty. Emphasize what they are already doing well, things they might do better, and how they might do that.

16. **Slip the punch.** It is important to know how to "slip a punch" and avoid a flat-out confrontation with students, particularly in the presence of other students. Try to defuse or redirect the student's energy by using patience. Avoid contradicting what an angry student says. Accepting feelings is not the same as agreeing with them.

17. **Avoid the escalator.** Some educators make the mistake of trying to enforce desired behavior by escalating threats of punishment. This can cause the educator to make threats that cannot be carried through (for example, "You are never coming back in this classroom!"). Work to remain calm by noting your own emotions and breathing deeply several times before choosing a response.

18. ***Use the moniker.*** Remember to use students' preferred names at every opportunity. A person's unique and personal name, when pronounced precisely and appropriately, can significantly influence relationships.

19. ***Be aware of paraverbal communication.*** The three paraverbal communication components are tone of voice, volume of voice, and the speed of talking. When working with an angry person, try to use a gentle tone of voice and a moderate volume, and speak more slowly. The way an educator responds to a person who is beginning to lose control can increase or decrease the likelihood of verbal or physical aggression.

20. ***Maintain a nonthreatening physical stance.*** An open body stance, with relaxed posture and your body slightly at an angle from the other person, will convey a message of compromise and conciliation. Avoid crossing arms, pointing fingers, or moving too close to the angry person. Give the other person personal space by adding distance between you.

21. ***Let them climb "emotion mountain."*** Where possible, when someone seeks to express a strong emotion, let the person vent without any interruption (lecturing, contradicting). Allowing the person to climb emotion mountain—to express feelings—sets the stage for dialogue. Blocking the climb only adds frustration.

These 21 suggestions are illustrative of the many ways educators who incorporate Invitational Education can help prevent school violence and encourage school safety. People turn to violence when socially acceptable avenues of expression are unavailable. It is imperative that schools send the signal to all students, in as many ways as possible, that they are able, valuable, responsible, and capable of acting accordingly.

SUMMARY

Because the "sun is not always shining" in schools, this chapter looked at how Invitational Education addresses difficult situations. A noncoercive perspective was provided to encourage safety in schools. Of particular use is the "6 Cs" approach introduced in this chapter. It demonstrates how to move from concern to conciliation in difficult situations. It serves as a framework for avoiding or managing conflicts. Twenty-one practical strategies showed the subtle but persistent strength of the inviting approach. Chapter 6 will look at intentional ways of developing this vital strength in those who wish to apply Invitational Education.

FURTHER REFLECTIONS AND ACTIVITIES

1. Think of ways that educators use rewards or consequences to get students or staff to do something. How might these requests be presented without the use of a reward or consequence? Consider approaches that provide a sense of autonomy, competence, and relatedness.

2. There are four steps in the 6 Cs of conflict management that precede the assignment of a consequence. Think about situations in your school where consequences are assigned as a first step. What benefits might there be in postponing the use of consequences? What message does it send to a student or colleague?

3. In what ways can an inviting stance of care, optimism, respect, and trust help educators to reach and form relationships with disengaged, isolated students? Identify students in your school who appear to be isolated, angry, or disconnected from peers. Brainstorm ways to demonstrate interest in and care for these students and share your successes. Consider identifying someone in the school who might serve as a dependable adult and mentor for each of these students.

CHAPTER 6

The Four Corner Press

Attention to the beliefs of teachers and teacher candidates should be a focus
for educational research and can inform educational practice in ways that
prevailing research agendas have not and cannot. (Pajares, 1992, p. 329)

As we have often noted, being intentionally inviting is both an ideal to reach
for and an evolving theory of practice to work with. This chapter looks
at the person in the process and considers what is necessary to sustain the
desire and energy to function at an intentionally inviting level—to develop
the stamina and courage of the long-distance inviter. Being professionally
inviting cannot be maintained if it is seen as an isolated series of behaviors
an educator performs when they come to school. Invitational Education
can easily be corrupted by those who have learned its techniques but not
its stance. As our colleague Charlotte Reed pointed out, "Invitational
Education is only one aspect of invitational living."

Living the inviting process involves orchestrating four basic areas: (1)
being personally inviting with oneself; (2) being personally inviting with
others; (3) being professionally inviting with oneself; and (4) being professionally inviting with others. The four arrows in Figure 6.1 represent the
stress caused by the constant demands for attention to the four dimensions.
The educator who successfully employs Invitational Education balances
these demands and integrates them into a seamless pattern of functioning.
Concentrating too much effort in only one or two of the four areas creates
an imbalance.

From an invitational viewpoint, a significant part of creating a socially
and emotionally safe climate is using oneself in creative and ethical ways.
The inviting educator can balance and orchestrate the demands of these
areas, thereby facilitating optimal personal and professional development
in oneself and others. These four areas suggest ways to increase one's "IQ"
(Invitational Quotient).

Figure 6.1. The Four Dimensions, a.k.a. The Four Corner Press

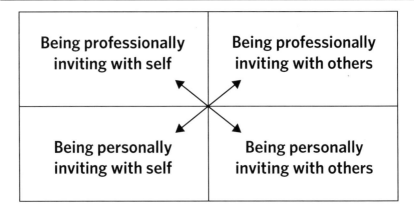

BEING PERSONALLY INVITING WITH ONESELF

> Many people go throughout life committing partial suicide—destroying their talents, energies, creative qualities. Indeed, to learn how to be good to oneself is often more difficult than to learn how to be good to others. (Liebman, 1946, p. 46)

Countless educators are dedicated, caring, and hardworking, but also experience chronic discouragement, dejection, and frustration. These feelings are summed up in the single word *burnout*, defined by Edelwich (1980) as the "progressive loss of idealism, energy, and purpose" (p. 14). Sometimes burnout is self-inflicted. Educators who overlook their own welfare are more likely to experience stress-induced illness. Avoiding boredom and isolation, principal components of burnout, is essential in maintaining an inviting stance.

Being an inviting educator does not require martyrdom. You have a perfect right to assert yourself.

Being an inviting educator does not require martyrdom. You have a perfect right to assert yourself. Your feelings are important. It's okay to let others know that you don't like something one bit. It's okay to express joy, sadness, and fear. These are part of being a human being.

When professionals constantly sacrifice their own wants and needs to meet the demands of others, the sacrifice gradually builds resentment. Teachers have a moral obligation to their students to take care of themselves. We have "a public duty" to preserve our own health. Thus, if one aspires to go the distance, to be a long-distance inviter, it is vital to view and treat oneself and one's potential positively.

Being personally inviting with oneself is a tremendously important enterprise for teachers. It is difficult to invite others if educators neglect to invite themselves. If educators believe that the inviting process is important, then they should apply this belief to their own lives—to stand tall, dress well, eat healthfully, become involved, exercise, take time to address your personal needs and interests, and find ways to be fully present in this world.

In being personally inviting with yourself, keep in mind that the principles of respect, optimism, trust, care, and intentionality most useful for inviting others also directly apply to inviting yourself. The most important principle is respect for yourself and your feelings. For example, if exercising at night after a hard day of teaching feels terribly difficult, try inviting yourself to exercise in the morning. If this doesn't work, a self-invitation to play a sport, join a health club, buy an exercise bicycle or mini-trampoline, or take a long walk each morning or evening might accomplish the same thing. The goal is to send self-invitations that are most likely to be accepted and acted upon. By listening to your own feelings and by varying self-invitations the probability of success is increased.

Although it is beyond the scope of this book to go into detail about the countless ways of being personally inviting with yourself, here are some suggestions for maintaining your own personal energy level and nurturing yourself physically, emotionally, and psychologically:

- *Take pleasure in stillness.* Too much isolation, as those living in quarantine as this book is in production know only too well, can be bad, but taking time to be alone is helpful. Enjoy silence. Contemplate and meditate on who you are, where you came from, and where you're going. Being at one with yourself can be deeply rewarding.
- *Practice Mindfulness.* Participate in a class in person or online, to learn how to incorporate a few minutes of mindfulness in your day. Mindfulness enables us to be calm and focused and able to respond rather than merely react to situations (Harris et al., 2017). The goal of mindfulness is not to rid your mind of thoughts, but instead to be able to be present with your thoughts without feeling the need to act on them immediately. Mindfulness practices support invitational living, as they help us to put space between strong stimuli and our response. It gives us time to let difficult emotions subside so we can then choose thoughtful actions. It also allows us to be fully present and appreciate the moment we are in so we can respond rather than react.
- *Keep in reasonable shape.* Maintain physical health. Whether you choose an individual effort (long walks, jogging, exercising, gardening) or an organized sport (bowling, tennis, racquetball), it

is important to maintain the body in which one lives. As the saying goes, "Where will you live if you don't take care of your body?"

- *Plan a long life.* Take personal responsibility for your own life support system. Be choosy about what and how much you eat and drink. Eliminate cigarettes and other injurious substances. Maintain health care, look both ways even when crossing a one-way street, and fasten your safety belt. The greatest proportion of health and safety care one receives is self-administered. You are your own primary care doctor. Learn to listen to Dr. You.
- *Give yourself a celebration.* Make a pledge to do something special for just yourself in the immediate future. It might be a bubble bath, a fishing expedition, a good novel, a shopping trip, a new outfit, a favorite meal, a round of golf, attending a film or play; celebrate!
- *Recharge your batteries.* Handle short-term burnout by talking things over with a trustworthy friend or counselor you consider to have good sense. Just talking about concerns helps avoid accepting a lot of guilt and anxiety. A good friend or professional counselor can help you find ways to invite yourself.
- *Live with a flourish.* Find satisfaction from many sources, such as a hobby or activity unrelated to your professional life. As much as realistically possible, surround yourself with things you like. Laugh a little. Take a few risks, travel, and assert yourself. Avoid drabness.
- *Accept new chapters in your life.* As we grow older it is important to focus on what we have, not what we don't have. Getting older requires adjustments to new ways of being and becoming. As you grow older, it seems important to remember that countless people are denied the privilege. Keep the spirit.

One additional way educators might invite themselves personally is by taking time to remember what it was like to be a child and letting their own feelings find expression. The death of a child is tragic, so why kill the child in yourself? Keep the zest for living alive by trusting your feelings, by being open to experience, by being gentle with yourself, and, when necessary, forgiving yourself. After all, errors are primarily sources of information. If one path does not take you where you wish to go, at least you've learned not to take that path again.

BEING PERSONALLY INVITING WITH OTHERS

The next important area in becoming a long-distance inviter is being personally inviting with others. Most human interactions have a basic process of interdependence. The greatest life support systems are relatives and friends, and Invitational Education places a high priority on personal relationships.

Professional success, no matter how great, cannot make up for lack of success in personal relationships. It is important to cultivate and treasure a circle of trusted friends and acquaintances as well as to seek out new relationships and explore fresh interests.

A most important aspect of inviting others personally is being "real." Disclosure begets disclosure, and it often helps to share personal feelings, to acknowledge that everyone wakes up on the wrong side of bed, speaks before thinking, and forgets appointments.

One additional aspect of inviting others personally is to develop and maintain unconditional regard and respect for other human beings. As discussed earlier, comments

> *Professional success, no matter how great, cannot make up for lack of success in personal relationships.*

or behaviors that are perceived by others as demeaning, insulting, sexist, homophobic, or racist are usually interpreted as disinviting regardless of one's intentions. Kidding others about their physical appearance, behavior, background, or misfortunes can be very disinviting. Saying "I was only kidding" may not be sufficient to repair the damage of a cruel jest. As someone commented, "Sticks and stones may break my bones, but words will surely kill me." Here are some practical ways to avoid lethal statements and to be personally inviting with others:

- *Promote civility.* Common courtesy is a most important tool in Invitational Education. This is usually accomplished by greeting others by appropriate name, showing respect by being prompt with appointments and commitments, promoting "please" and "thank you," and in general demonstrating basic concern and appreciation for others and their feelings.
- *Let people know you care.* Often a get-well card is sent to those who are ill, but a welcome-back note is overlooked. A thoughtful birthday, holiday, congratulatory, or other card or note to relatives, colleagues, students, and friends lets them know that they are in your thoughts. Consider writing a note by hand instead of sending a text or email. The time you took to do so will be especially appreciated.
- *Warm up the class.* At the beginning of each class period, a personal greeting, a little light humor, a brief comment on world events, or an inquiry into how things are going can set the stage for learning. Just as joggers should limber up their muscles before jogging, teachers should limber up their classes before teaching. Take note of any student who might seem distressed or disengaged. They may be experiencing strong emotions about something that happened prior to class. Find a way to check in with them privately.

- *Break bread together.* One of the oldest forms of community is sharing a bit of food and drink. By arranging for something during break or other appropriate times, you set the stage for facilitating good feelings and friendships. As one of the authors learned, someone asking if you would like some tea is often an invitation to sit, relax, and talk.
- *Keep things simple.* When someone comes with a complaint, avoid second-level problems, such as an angry exchange or countercomplaints. Focus on what the person is saying, listen carefully, and be willing to express regret (this is not the same as an apology). If possible, take some positive action to let the person know that at least you listened and understood their feelings.
- *Stay abreast of current events and culture.* Make a special effort to get a sense of the world in which today's student lives. Keep abreast of contemporary fads, fashions, heroes, films, sports, actors, singers, and other current student interests. Using an example from real life can be both personally and professionally inviting. On the other hand, being playfully out of it can be a way to have a good cross-generational conversation.

Positive beliefs about people, coupled with personally inviting behaviors, are basic to Invitational Education. Yet, as important as it is to be personally inviting with oneself and others, it takes even more effort and skill to become professionally inviting. This leads to the next two areas—being professionally inviting with oneself and being professionally inviting with others.

BEING PROFESSIONALLY INVITING WITH ONESELF

It is difficult to overestimate the importance of being active in one's own professional development. The educator who does not invite himself or herself to grow professionally runs the risk of becoming obsolete. Teachers should continue to be actively engaged in upgrading their skills and knowledge and working to sustain their professional enthusiasm.

Teachers can grow professionally in many ways. Especially challenging is to develop a philosophy of teaching. Teachers can get locked into certain habits of teaching, especially if they have experienced some success with it. Being in a rut, even a successful one, narrows perspective and diminishes professional vitality. Consider using Invitational Education as a framework for your teaching philosophy. This will assist you greatly in evaluating the many instructional strategies that you come across and help you decide if they align with an inviting stance. The following list represents suggestions for discovering fresh approaches to being professionally inviting with yourself:

- *Participate in programs.* In addition to typical academic courses, programs, and degrees, special conferences and workshops can provide exciting ways to sharpen skills, learn techniques, and develop new understandings. Attending such professional activities will help upgrade skills and knowledge. You can often find funds to attend developmental activities by contacting PTAs, governmental agencies, business partners, and philanthropic foundations.

- *Spend time reading.* Countless professional books, journals, magazine articles, newsletters, and monographs are expressly written to help educators develop professionally. In today's busy world, viewing webinars and listening to brief podcasts while commuting to work are easy ways to learn something new and reflect on your practice. Finding some time each day to read and listen is an excellent way to stay current in your profession.

- *Join professional groups.* Be active in professional societies. Working within these organizations to ensure that they maintain high professional quality is important in strengthening yourself professionally as well as aiding the profession. A nonprofit organization that we highly recommend is the International Alliance for Invitational Education. For information, visit www. invitationaleducation.net or see Appendix A.

- *Conduct action research projects.* Some educators might assume that research should be left to scientists in laboratories, surrounded by computers and data sheets. But bigger is not necessarily better. A teacher's quiet investigation of some question can have a long-range influence on life in and around schools.

- *Write papers.* A valuable way to invite yourself professionally is to write for professional publication. Not everything written must appear in national journals. Numerous local, state, and regional newsletters, journals, and related publications welcome contributions from educators in the field.

- *Arrange a date.* Are there people in your professional world whom you admire and would like to know better? If so, be brave! Invite them to join you for a cup of coffee or to have lunch together. If you invite, they may accept. If you don't invite, they can't. Some people develop their own podcasts as a way to meet and interview influential people.

- *Seek feedback.* At regular intervals and at the end of each semester seek suggestions from students or others who may be familiar with your work. Find out how they evaluate your teaching and what you might do to make it better. This way you can be showing respect for the opinions of others while strengthening yourself professionally.

- *Take an online course:* There is a plethora of possibilities for professional development available online. Take a course in your area of expertise or explore a new subject or skill. Anytime you learn something new, you become a better teacher. The Great Courses program and Coursera provide myriad ways to keep learning.

Personal and professional growth ultimately culminates in being better able to be professionally inviting with others.

BEING PROFESSIONALLY INVITING WITH OTHERS

Students' perceptions of themselves as learners apparently serve as personal guidance systems to direct their classroom behavior.

From the position advocated in this book, the primary purpose of education is to summon people cordially to realize their potential, meet the democratic needs of society, and participate in the progress of civilization. This is best accomplished by building on the three areas already considered. When these three are functioning at an optimal level, the stage is set for being professionally inviting with others.

Because the process of being professionally inviting with others is the central focus of this book, it is necessary to go into greater detail in this area. The examination of the fourth area uses self-concept as a springboard.

Earlier, reviewed evidence indicated a significant relationship between self-concept and school achievement. Students' perceptions of themselves as learners apparently serve as personal guidance systems to direct their classroom behavior. A professional understanding of self-concept theory coupled with skills for interpreting how students view themselves as learners are important tools for teaching.

The Florida Key

In 1973 Purkey, Cage, and Graves developed The Florida Key, a survey designed to measure student self-concept-as-learner. Since its creation, the Key has been revised and adapted numerous times. In later adaptations it became the Inviting Teacher Survey (ITS; Amos & Purkey, 1988; Ripley, 1986) and the Invitational Online Teaching Assessment (IOTA; Lockwood et al., 2014.) The IOTA was designed for use by teachers of online courses and is available for FREE at http://invitationaledonline.com. Although the original Key is over 40 years old, it does identify four factors that appear to relate to how students feel about themselves as learners. The four factors are relating, asserting, investing, and coping.

The Key limits itself to the situation-specific self-concept that seems to relate most closely to school success or failure: self-as-learner. In making deductions about self-concept, most researchers have focused on global self-concepts rather than on situation-specific self-images, such as self as athlete, self as family member, self as learner, or self as friend. By observing only global self-concept—which is multifaceted and contains diverse, even conflicting sub-selves—investigators have sometimes overlooked the importance of these subsystems.

In the Key research, four factors that relate significantly to school performance were derived through factor analysis. These factors were labeled (1) relating, (2) asserting, (3) investing, and (4) coping. Examining these four factors is useful, for they suggest ways in which educators may be professionally inviting with others.

Relating

The first factor identified on the Key as having the greatest significance to the self as learner is relating. As measured by the Key, the relating score indicates the level of trust and appreciation that the student maintains toward others.

Students who score high in relating identify closely with classmates, teachers, and school. They express positive feelings about learning, and they think in terms of our school, our teachers, and my classmates (as opposed to the teacher, that school, or those kids). Getting along with others is easy for those who score high on relating. These students take a natural, relaxed approach to school life. They stay calm when things go wrong, and they can express feelings of frustration or impatience without exploding.

Students who score low on relating seem unable to involve themselves in school activities or with teachers and other students. One teacher depicted such a student as follows:

Two summers ago, I tutored children who were having problems learning to read. Looking back, I can see how their reading problems were related to how they saw themselves. One boy, John, who was 10 years old, was not well-liked because of his habit of criticizing others to make himself feel important. His poor self-concept and failure to relate to others were graphically illustrated one day when a huge whipped cream fight was held on an empty hilltop. Whipped cream filled the air for 20 minutes or so as 40 kids, each with two or three cans, went wild. After the cream had settled, and later that day, John told me he had to spray whipped cream on himself as no one else made a point of doing so.

To be ignored, even in a whipped cream battle, can be a most painful experience.

To be overlooked or ignored by others is an intolerable situation for most people, and they will go to great lengths to gain acceptance. When the desire for positive human relationships is unfulfilled in conventional ways, students are likely to try less conventional ways or socially unacceptable ways. For example, a young person may join a gang to gain a feeling of status or acceptance denied by the larger society. Alcohol and drugs are used socially, as well as by chronic heavy drinkers and addicts, to reduce feelings of personal failure, isolation, and worthlessness.

> *When the desire for positive human relationships is unfulfilled in conventional ways, students are likely to try less conventional ways or socially unacceptable ways.*

Substance abuse of all kinds has increased at alarming rates. According to the National Center for Health Statistics (Hedegaard et al., 2017) there were more than 63,600 deaths due to drug overdose in the United States in 2016—an increase from 6.1% per 100,000 people in 1999 to 19.8% in 2016. Of national concern is the role of opioids (both prescription and illicit) in overdose deaths. Opioids were involved in 42,249 deaths in 2016—five times more than in 1999. If all schools made relationship-centered environments a priority, more young adults would develop the perceptions and skills they need to avoid becoming a statistic.

The following passage from *Manchild in the Promised Land*, Claude Brown's 1965 portrayal of the harsh realities of growing up in Harlem in the 1940s and 1950s, illustrates the pathetic efforts of one young girl to buy human relationships and the willingness of others to exploit those efforts:

> I found out that Sugar would bring candy and pickles to class and give them to Carole, so Carole liked her and wanted me to like her too. . . Sugar started coming around on the weekends, and she always had money and wanted to take me to the show. Sometimes I would go with Sugar, and sometimes I would just take her money and go with somebody else. Most of the time I would take Sugar's money then find Bucky and take him to the show. . . I never could get rid of Sugar. She would follow me around all day long and would keep trying to give me things, and when I didn't take them, she would start looking real pitiful and say she didn't want me to have it anyway. The only way I could be nice to Sugar was to take everything she had, so I started being real nice to her. (p. 55)

Literary descriptions as well as scientific research clearly show that human relationships profoundly influence self-concept and school achievement. Although forcing students to relate to each other in positive and productive ways is undesirable and probably impossible, teachers can create an enabling atmosphere in which relating is facilitated.

A specific teacher behavior that invites feelings of belonging in students is the use of "we" statements to suggest group membership. Encouraging students to involve themselves in school activities promotes a feeling of *our* curriculum, *our* decorations, *our* rules, *our* efforts to keep things clean. Instructional programs can be developed and presented in ways that encourage students to play a cooperative part.

Finally, creating the proper atmosphere for relating involves removing barriers. Skill is necessary to avoid a mismatch between the communication system of the classroom and that of a particular group. Teachers may be unintentionally disinviting when they appear to be condescending, patronizing, or overly friendly. "That English teacher tries to be helpful," a student commented, "but she always talks about how 'you Blacks can be proud of what you've done.' It shows me that she is constantly aware of the differences and thinks in terms of labels."

One of the author's students made a telling point when he said: "No matter how smart or educated you are, you can teach me nothing if I think you are racist, sexist, or homophobic." Teachers who want to be inviting with others work to avoid expressions and actions likely to be offensive. This requires sensitivity to how things seem from the other person's point of view. Teachers who understand the importance of relating, work to remove barriers and to encourage positive relationships in the classroom.

Asserting

> That which gave me most uneasiness among those Maids of Honor, when my Nurse carried me to visit them, was to see them use me without any Matter of Ceremony, like a Creature who had no Sort of Consequence.
>
> —Jonathan Swift, *Gulliver's Travels*, 1726

The second factor identified in the Key research, *asserting*, describes another aspect of self-concept-as-learner—the one that characterizes students' sense of control over what happens to them in the classroom. Students who score high on the asserting factor speak up for their own ideas and are not afraid to ask questions in class. They actively participate in school activities and talk to others about their academic interests.

The importance of asserting oneself has been stressed by Alberti & Emmons (1990), who define assertive behavior as those personal actions that enable one to act in one's own best interests, to stand up for oneself without undue anxiety, to express one's honest feelings comfortably, and to exercise one's own rights without denying the rights of others. Alberti and Emmons view assertive behavior as affirming one's own rights (in contrast to aggressive behavior, which is directed against others) and the "perfect right" of every individual in interpersonal relationships. Beyond affirming one's own rights, assertive behavior also involves the ability to express feelings of positive regard, appreciation, and love—to let others know their presence invites a celebration.

One small subgroup of students often overlooked in the professional literature has very little difficulty in asserting itself, the class clown. In a book on class clowns by one of the authors (Purkey, 2006), evidence is presented that a distinguishing characteristic of class clowns is that they insist on asserting themselves. (This is no surprise to most teachers.) The secret of teaching class clowns is to use their assertive qualities in positive ways. Enjoy the lightheartedness and fun. Teaching is too important to take seriously. Some of them will grow up and become famous comedians. For a detailed study of class clowns, see *Teaching Class Clowns (And What They Can Teach Us)* (Purkey, 2006).

Advantages of assertive behavior have been documented by research (Purkey, 2006). Seligman (1975, 2006, 2011), who has formulated theories of learned optimism and learned helplessness, states that the experience of internal control is essential to both positive self-esteem and good psychological health. Negative self-regard and psychological depression are the likely results of feelings of helplessness. The problem with learned helplessness is that when one learns to believe that one lacks control, this belief persists even when circumstances have altered so that it does become possible to assert oneself. As Seligman has documented, optimists do better in school and succeed more at life tasks. One's optimistic feelings of control over what happens to oneself as a student are strongly related to school success.

Assertive behavior can be learned; it can be taught by teachers who invite dialogue and expression of different viewpoints in the classroom and who respect the students' right to express these viewpoints. Class activities that stress moral reasoning, democratic decisionmaking, and cultural appreciation promote assertive behavior. Many teachers have used such activities to encourage students to explore their own values, rights, and responsibilities.

Teachers can also encourage assertive behavior in their students by teaching them how to express themselves in socially acceptable ways without aggressing against others or denying others' rights. Some children learn to assert themselves early, as evidenced by the words of a little girl overheard on a playground: "Just because I don't know how to jump doesn't mean that I always have to turn the rope!" Significant differences exist between assertion and aggression. Both teachers and students benefit when they understand these differences and employ assertion rather than aggression in interpersonal relationships. When students are encouraged to assert themselves in socially acceptable ways, their feelings about themselves and their abilities are likely to improve along with their academic performance.

A way to encourage student assertion is to teach students how to avoid or bypass roadblocks to learning. A big problem for many students, especially those who are highly anxious, is what to do when they do not know the correct answer. In oral reading, a student who does not know a word will usually stammer, stutter, and suffer painful pauses until the teacher or another student supplies the answer. Much of this effort is counterproductive and can sometimes be avoided if the teacher invites students to jump over the difficult problem and keep going. In oral reading, for example, the student can bypass the unknown word by replacing it with the words *hard word* and keep going. In a multiple-choice test, the student can be told to select an option and move on. The important thing for a student is not to get blocked or hung up on an endless regression that often leads to lowered performance and self-confidence.

> Contrary to the standard advice that "If it's worth doing, it's worth doing well," encouraging students to do things poorly, at least in the beginning, may be helpful. Doing things well results from first doing things poorly.

One final method useful in encouraging students to assert themselves is to show them that going from something to something is much easier than going from nothing to something. By getting started, even if the start is poor, students begin their journey toward improvement and quality outcomes. Contrary to the standard advice that "If it's worth doing, it's worth doing well," encouraging students to do things poorly, at least in the beginning, may be helpful. Doing things well results from first doing things poorly. Being afraid to do things poorly leads to being afraid to do things at all.

Investing

The third factor identified by the Key research is the creative part of self-concept-as-learner: *investing*. This factor encompasses student willingness to speculate, guess, and try new things. Students who score high in investing seek out things to do in school without the prompting of extrinsic rewards such as tokens, gold stars, grades, points, or praise. Their reward appears to be the activity itself. Teachers can encourage students to invest themselves in learning by posing open-ended questions.

Open-ended questions do more than require students to regurgitate known facts. Open-ended questions are varied and interesting and ask students to interpret meanings, give opinions, compare and contrast ideas, or combine facts to form general principles. Here are a few examples: What would it be like if we were all born with only two fingers on each hand? What if the South had won the Civil War? What if the earth's axis shifted five degrees? What if the supply of oil were exhausted? What if a license were required to have a child? What if the world became a one-party democracy? Or, even more simply, "What is justice?" "Loyalty?" "Happiness?" "Truth?" Or, more complexly, "Why is there something rather than nothing?" Such questions can stir student imagination, create excitement in the classroom, and encourage all students to invest themselves in the discussions. Asking provocative, open-ended questions is an excellent way to summon student investment in learning, particularly when the questions are followed by sufficient wait-time. There is no one answer to an open-ended question, and, when the teacher accepts all explorations, more students will risk sharing their responses. Good questions can even lead to better questions from students. Dependably inviting teachers use a variety of methods to encourage investing.

Investing behaviors can also be called forth by having students do assignments in two different ways. For example, in doing a book report, students can be asked to look at the story from the point of view of at least three characters. This also helps with perspective-taking, an important part of being a socially developing person.

Coping

Coping, the fourth and final factor identified by the Key research, indicates how well students seem to be meeting school requirements. Students who score high in this area apparently possess an image of themselves as able and willing to meet aacademic expectations, as well as the social and emotional pressures that are ever growing for today's youth. They believe in their own academic ability and take pride in their classroom performance. They usually pay attention in class, do their work with care, finish what they start, and expect success from their efforts. They are able to respond to life's stresses in healthy ways. Students who score high in coping have discovered and use two important tools of learning: reading and journaling. They often pursue these activities independently, even when they are not required. Keeping a journal provides an outlet for reflective thinking about our experiences, emotions, and ideas, and builds self-awareness.

Coping is another name for school success, a subject emphasized throughout this book. What has not been sufficiently emphasized is that no single factor is more relevant to feelings of coping than the act of coping itself. By successfully coping with school expectations, students develop a sense of competence. "I know I can spell," an elementary school student wrote. "I got a good note one time." This sense of competence is a significant part of positive self-regard.

The feeling of competence gained through doing something that works is particularly valuable for children in the elementary grades. When children are successful at leading a class activity, giving a weather report, passing out material, taking attendance, or storing playground equipment, they are using learned skills to do things that work.

Things that work in higher grades include planning and preparing a dinner in a home and career class, plotting points on a parking lot in a math class, taking a leadership role in a service learning project, reading a French menu in a foreign language class, or executing a double reverse in football. One student described the process of learning something that works as follows:

> My first 2 years at school I was terrible at physical education. "Any girl can kick better than you," I was told. I was always picked last for kickball teams because I could not kick the ball into the air (a firm rule was no grounders). On one particular day in 3rd grade, my teacher, who was sitting with another teacher watching the game, saw that I was soon about to take my turn and undoubtedly kick grounders until I was out. This lady (all 6 feet of her) called me aside and showed me how to kick under the ball. When I got up to kick, the ball sailed in the air! I'll always remember that teacher who took the time to show me that I could do something that works!

Any honest success experience, no matter how small or in what area, helps students discover that they can cope with life's expectations. There are times, of course, when students are not coping and it is necessary to point out their errors. But teachers should not view this as an inconsequential act. "Pointing out mistakes, as John Dewey believed, 'should not wither the sources of creative insight. Before individuals can produce significant things, they must first produce'" (cited in Hook, 1939, p. 19). The stress from fear of failure makes it difficult for children to take the risk of learning. In the classroom, this means that to do things well, students must first do. Dependably inviting teachers recognize that experience emerges from inexperience, and that learning is a process of trying things out and finding what works and what does not.

Rather than focusing on mistakes and criticizing poor performance, teachers who are dependably inviting encourage students to feel confident in coping with errors and overcoming them. One high school girl told how this was accomplished for her:

> I was being auditioned for a part in our high-school musical. I was very nervous and worried about getting the part. At the end of my song my voice cracked and I thought my acting and singing days were over. The director looked at me and smiled, saying 'Let's just hope you hit that note on opening night.' It was definitely the warmest feeling I've ever experienced."

When students understand that making mistakes is normal, expected, and understandable, they can develop positive and realistic self-concepts as learners. Carol Dweck's research in self-theories (2000) underscores the importance of fostering a growth mindset in both students and educators. People who have a growth mindset are "mastery-oriented" learners. They "love learning, seek challenges, value effort, and persist in the face of obstacles." As mentioned earlier in Chapter 2, a growth mindset helps them to view mistakes simply as a signal to try a different strategy, instead of as proof of incompetence.

The four factors of the Florida Key—relating, asserting, investing, and coping—identify techniques that teachers can use to enable students to develop positive self-concepts as learners and encourage academic achievement.

SUMMARY

Chapter 6 has highlighted the importance of the person in the process of creating and maintaining a more humane school climate. Four basic areas of functioning were presented: being personally inviting with oneself, being personally inviting with others, being professionally inviting with oneself, and being professionally inviting with others. The successful educator is one who artfully blends and synchronizes these four areas and can thus sustain the energy and enthusiasm of the long-distance inviter. This chapter concluded by identifying practical strategies for creating and maintaining a positive climate while encouraging academic achievement. In the next chapter we examine how to invite change using the Invitational HELIX.

FURTHER REFLECTIONS AND ACTIVITIES

1. What do you like to do that no one makes you do? During the next week, keep a log of the personally inviting things you do and note your thoughts and feelings during these activities. Do they help you to feel refreshed, energized, or positively connected to others? On busy days, try to do at least one personally inviting thing, even for just a few minutes.

2. Do you have a student or colleague that lacks confidence or assertiveness? Make a list of things you can do to help them develop these social skills. Try out your strategies and note any changes in behavior and attitude over time.

3. The next time you are struggling with a task, pay attention to your "self-talk"—what are you saying to yourself about your effort and level of success? What positive, supportive things did you hear? What discouraging comments were you thinking?

During the next month, provide your students with opportunities to monitor their own "self-talk" (what they say to themselves) when doing a task. Begin with a task that is easy to do (like a simple puzzle). Working in pairs, have one student say out loud what they are thinking and telling themselves while performing the task, while their partner writes their comments down. Then, repeat the experience with a more challenging task. Ask the note-taking students to share some of the positive and negative comments they heard. This activity helps students (and colleagues) to recognize how self-talk influences what we believe to be true about our abilities, our level of effort, and our response to challenges.

CHAPTER 7

The Invitational HELIX

> Community is the tie that binds students and teachers together in special ways, to something more significant than themselves: shared values, and ideals. It lifts both teachers and students to higher levels of self-understanding, commitment, and performance—beyond the reaches of the shortcomings and difficulties they face in their everyday lives. Community can help teachers and students be transformed from a collection of "I's" to a collective "we," thus providing them with a unique and enduring sense of identity, belonging, and place. (Sergiovanni, 1994, p. xiii)

When it comes to creating inviting schools, there is good news and bad news for those developing intentionally inviting schools. First the bad news: There is no guaranteed lock-step method for ensuring a safe and inviting school, because each school, like each family, has its own unique characteristics. To impose a standard form on all schools would be to miss the living qualities that make each school unique. Now the good news: Presently, more than 450 schools and universities have received the Inviting School Award for successfully using Invitational Education to create, maintain, and sustain a positive school climate. Over 90 of these schools and universities have received the Inviting School Fidelity Award. This prestigious award is presented to those institutions that have maintained their commitment to Invitational Education for over 10 years.

From an analysis of these and other experiences, a cumulative 12-step plan of action for creating inviting schools, called HELIX, has been developed. (The HELIX will be explained in more detail later in this chapter.) To assist schools in their Invitational Education journey through the steps of the HELIX, the International Alliance for Invitational Education has created the 12-step Invitational Education Toolkit: a comprehensive professional development program. The Invitational Education Toolkit includes slide presentations, detailed facilitation notes, handouts for workshop and meeting participants, activities, video clips, and professional support. Designed to help any educator lead their school through a successful implementation, the Invitational Education Toolkit provides a dynamic path to reflective practice, positive action, and sustainable change.

The purpose of the HELIX is to provide a clear roadmap to measure the progress of a school in creating and maintaining a positive school culture. By analogy, the HELIX is like a ladder. It encourages one step at a time in improving school climate. The HELIX reminds its users that understanding, and successful application, of Invitational Education takes time and effort.

Founded by William Purkey and Betty Siegel in 1982, The International Alliance for Invitational Education (IAIE) hosts an interactive website, https://www.invitationaleducation.net, that provides a wealth of information, resources, and services to assist you in your invitational journey. The Inviting School Award Program offers a unique opportunity for schools to receive international recognition for their accomplishments in creating an inviting climate. The program includes the Inviting School Survey-Revised, which provides a school with disaggregated data about the perceptions stakeholders have regarding the school's people, places, policies, programs, and processes. IAIE also serves as a worldwide network for schools interested in and practicing Invitational Education. Through the alliance you may contact other schools to learn about their school climate strategies and even arrange for school visits and exchange programs. Please visit https://www.invitationaleducation.net for more about these Invitational Education tools, services, and programs. Let's now look in more depth at the HELIX.

> *The purpose of the HELIX is to provide a clear roadmap to measure the progress of a school in creating and maintaining a positive school culture.*

USING THE INVITATIONAL HELIX

Creating an inviting school involves an awareness and understanding of the theory presented in this book, the application of this theory to real situations, and a commitment by those involved to work together to realize shared goals. Coordinating these efforts on a schoolwide basis requires making sense of many different working parts and understanding how each part works progressively to create an intentionally inviting school.

This chapter introduces a guidance system called the HELIX (Purkey & Novak, 1993), which was developed in response to calls for more complex analyses of Invitational Education and for greater emphasis on the deeper ethical and democratic implications of the inviting process. A clear vision of what the school wants to accomplish, and why, is the hallmark of a good school. Usually, this vision consists of a theory of practice that is understood and shared by everyone in the school. This chapter presents such a vision and provides a roadmap to success that can be understood by everyone in the school.

The Invitational HELIX is a practical guide for educators seeking to create and sustain an inviting school in which practice deepens over time. The HELIX is based on the idea that for educators to use an invitational framework they have to move from being aware of it, to understanding it, to applying it, and finally to being committed to adopting it and keeping it going. Thus, using an inviting perspective involves four stages: awareness, understanding, application, and adoption. In addition, schools can be at different phases in employing Invitational Education. Some schools may be merely seeking to introduce some inviting practices; others may wish to apply Invitational Education in a systematic way. Still others wish to have it as their pervasive philosophy. With this progression of purposes in mind, three phases have been identified depending on the school's degree of commitment: occasional, systematic, and pervasive. The HELIX spirals through four stages while progressing through three phases. Its 12-step guide enables practitioners to identify at what stage and phase their school is presently functioning and what is the next higher step in becoming an inviting school.

Although a plethora of bandwagons for educational change seem to exist, most do not get at the deep structures of schools. Using the Invitational HELIX is a way to build on Invitational Education's intuitive appeal and take it to progressively higher phases. Let's look at each phase and step of the HELIX, which is a diagram designed to illustrate the process of creating an inviting school (see Figure 7.1).

OCCASIONAL INTEREST (PHASE I)

All schools are inviting in some ways at some times. The beginning phase of the Invitational HELIX aims at helping people in a school recognize and sustain current practices that are inviting and try out some new ways of doing things. This initial phase provides beginning level exposure to Invitational Education, encourages some awareness of its terminology, and identifies ways to introduce inviting practices within the school. Staff members explore how their mindsets and messages positively or negatively influence what others believe to be true about themselves. They are encouraged to experiment with using more caring, optimistic, respectful, and trustworthy words and actions.

What marks this phase as the beginning level is that it is characterized by a variety of suggestions for new inviting practices that are only tangentially

> *The beginning phase of the Invitational HELIX aims at helping people in a school recognize and sustain current practices that are inviting and try out some new ways of doing things.*

Figure 7.1. The Invitational HELIX

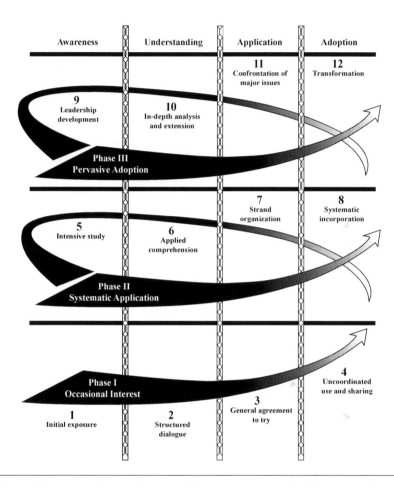

related. The suggestions often provide attention to and affirmation of methods and skills already in practice in the school. These suggestions are nonthreatening, generally unrelated to each other, and relatively easy to apply.

Phase I processes are concerned with creating an inviting ambiance within the school, which might include changing signs on buildings, hanging plants in the foyer, answering telephones differently, finding ways to improve communication, acknowledging student and staff efforts and initiatives, or organizing social events. Although positive, these introductory activities bring about little change in the deep structure of the school. They are, however, important in themselves and prepare the school for higher levels of inviting.

Phase I is also about the renewal of the educational spirit in a school—about doing education in the right way for the right reasons. It's important during this phase that people are asked to remember why they came into education and what makes it worth it now.

Initial Exposure (Step 1)

This first step deals with a beginning awareness of Invitational Education. This initial exposure might take place while educators are attending a conference or workshop, hearing a speaker, reading an article or book (such as this one), talking with colleagues, or viewing a video. Acknowledging that Invitational Education is not only about creating a positive climate for students and parents, but also about aiding staff members in realizing *their* potential, sends an important message to school adults about their ability and value. Ideally, this dawning of awareness is an enjoyable experience that prepares staff members for the interactions necessary in the next step.

Structured Dialogue (Step 2)

Good ideas gain additional meaning when they are shared. This second step involves some form of organized discussion within the school, to deepen understanding about what it means for something or someone to be inviting. This might be an afternoon meeting following a general session program, a retreat, a series of team or job-alike meetings, or other type of organized discussion on ways to apply Invitational Education within the school. Although the emphasis at this step is on understanding the inviting approach, this understanding is enhanced by recognizing and appreciating practices already taking place in the school that are clearly inviting. Participants in the dialogue at this step can explain why certain practices may be perceived as inviting or disinviting. Probing into why leads to a better understanding of the underlying dynamics of the approach. During this process, participants may identify initiatives that are time consuming and perhaps perceived in conflicting ways by stakeholders. As part of Step 4, a discussion may follow to decide if the initiative should be disbanded, making room for new efforts. Asking staff members to share one or two things that would make them feel more valued and respected in the school can lead to greater buy-in and interest in exploring the invitational framework further.

General Agreement to Try (Step 3)

This next step takes people from structured dialogue to a general consensus among school members to try various inviting ideas, collectively or individually. This is still the beginning phase, so these trials typically consist of uncoordinated individual or small-group efforts. The purpose of Step 3 is to try out new ideas and see what works. A discussion of what works is very important for incorporating new practices and beliefs into daily practice. In this step, small modifications and innovations, such as making signs more positively worded, highlighting innovative staff projects and student work, sending appreciation cards, addressing a procedure that has been causing difficulties for staff members, or trying an inviting approach to a challenging student or parent conference are expected and welcome. Members leave this meeting with something they are excited about, agree to put it into practice, and set up a time to talk about how it went.

Uncoordinated Use and Sharing (Step 4)

The beginning phase of the Invitational HELIX concludes with opportunities to share feedback on new initiatives in order for them to be understood, appreciated, and improved. At this step, people report what is working, what is challenging, and what should be abandoned. Successful practices become part of everyday school practice. Publicly affirming what is working within both the school and community sets the stage for discussions about deeper commitments regarding Invitational Education. Recognizing successes prepares the ground for advanced levels of practice.

SYSTEMATIC APPLICATION (PHASE II)

After people in a school have heard about, discussed, tried, and successfully applied some inviting practices, they then develop relationships among these various practices to produce integrative change within the school. Integrative change happens when people are willing to work together to systematically affect practices in the whole school. Educators look beyond their own classrooms, their own offices, and their own students to try to develop a mutually satisfiable way to make the school operation a shared enterprise.

> *The sense that "we are in this together" takes hold during the systematic application phase as people look at the school as a whole and work in groups to develop inviting places, policies, programs, and processes.*

The sense that "we are in this together" takes hold during the systematic application phase as people look at the school as a whole and work in groups to develop inviting places, policies, programs, and processes. In this phase also, students, parents, and members of the community are encouraged to become involved in examining, proposing, implementing, and evaluating suggestions for improvement. For these systematic activities to work, members of the school seek to create an atmosphere that intentionally manifests trust, respect, optimism, and care.

Intensive Study (Step 5)

Because educators are now seeking to apply Invitational Education in a systematic way, they need an awareness of Invitational Education as a system. And so, this step is characterized by systematic study of Invitational Education. School members need to become aware of the various components of Invitational Education to gain a deeper understanding of its foundations, elements, domains, levels, and dimensions. An Illustration of Invitational Theory (Figure 3.1) provides a helpful overview. This systematic study should be directed by an experienced and knowledgeable person who has a sound background in, and commitment to, Invitational Education. Step 5 requires careful reading over a period of time and may involve a full-day intensive workshop (or series of shorter workshops) and follow-up.

Fundamentals of Invitational Education, 2nd Edition (Purkey & Novak, 2016) provides a brief introduction to Invitational Education and was designed as a quick read for school faculties and staff. As staff members become intrigued by how inviting practices can help them both personally and professionally, we recommend engaging in a book study using this book, *Developing Inviting Schools,* which provides more detail about the components of the theory.

Applied Comprehension (Step 6)

Comprehension of the systemic nature of Invitational Education means that those involved at this step are able to relate theoretical concepts to actual issues in the school. At this step those involved make efforts to explain their understanding of Invitational Education, to reflect on what is presently happening in the school, and to compare what is taking place in light of what is desirable. It is here that the 5 Ps are used to think about what might need to be addressed to make the school a more integrated inviting place. Parents and community partners may be asked to share their perceptions.

Strand Organization (Step 7)

This step introduces the 5-P Relay, created by William Purkey. A detailed, step-by-step description can be found in *Creating a Positive School Climate* (Purkey, 2017). In this systematic approach to brainstorming, evaluating, and implementing new practices, all stakeholders are asked to join one of five "strands" corresponding to the 5 Ps (People, Places, Policies, Programs, and Processes). Strand members may include students, parents, clerical staff, teacher assistants, aides and monitors, custodians, and food-service professionals in addition to teachers and administrators. Each strand takes one of the 5 Ps (People, Places, Policies, Programs, and Processes) as a home base. A rotation method is then used so that all strands will have input into each strand's goals, procedures, obstacles and barriers, evaluation, and refinement. A coordinator for each strand is appointed and general consensus is reached with the strand members about the priority of the goals to be pursued.

Systematic Incorporation (Step 8)

With the strands working as operational units (often with their own name and logo), the goal of this step is to institutionalize the 5 P strands and their work throughout the school. This involves regular strand meetings, coordinator meetings, feedback to all members of the school community, and special efforts to keep things going. In addition, networks may be formed with other schools and organizations and plans made for long-term staff development. By the conclusion of this step, the school has made significant progress toward developing an inviting culture.

PERVASIVE ADOPTION (PHASE III)

Schools are complex organizations in which many things are tried, but only a select few are retained to become part of the operating culture. The goal of Phase III is to have Invitational Education pervade the entire fabric of the school and beyond. In other words, Invitational Education becomes internalized in the institutional norms and "the way things are done here." This requires sustained dialogue about the assumptions of Invitational Education and the continued development of a community where democratic leadership flourishes. The school becomes a place where everyone works together so that what's good gets done. As a result of this participation, a school will have many leaders who can use Invitational Education as a creative and sustained heuristic to examine and deal with issues of personal, professional, institutional, and societal importance.

Not only are members of the school community congenial and civil, they are also collegial. They respect each other's intentions and competence, and they make concerted efforts to learn from, and with, one another. Members of this learning community become invitational leaders, and their schools are seen as exemplary models of Invitational Education. These individuals and schools take a proactive stance that incorporates, explores, and extends the deepest intellectual and ethical commitments of the inviting perspective.

Leadership Development (Step 9)

An appreciation of the complexity of Invitational Education develops as emerging leaders formally explore the relationship between Invitational Education and other school goals. This may result in developing or reconceptualizing the school's mission statement.

By taking on a more inviting stance, educators become more intentional in the choices they make and the processes they use when addressing challenges, needs, and projects. Command and control is replaced by cooperation and communication. Subordinates become associates, and everyone in the school is provided opportunities to lead. Members of the 5-P strands explore larger projects to support learning, leading, and living.

The International Alliance for Invitational Education provides an international forum for discussing both theory and practice.

In-Depth Analysis and Extension (Step 10)

Leaders in Invitational Education are asked to critically analyze Invitational Education and to compare and contrast it with other school improvement approaches. An even deeper understanding is demonstrated by the ability to translate other approaches into acceptable or unacceptable practices from an inviting perspective. New initiatives are analyzed from an inviting perspective to see if there is:

- a focus on a person's perspective;
- an emphasis on self-concept-as-learner;
- an evaluation of humane effectiveness;
- an action orientation toward school safety; and
- an encouragement of democratic deliberation.

Answering these questions enables practitioners of Invitational Education to be both prudent and constructive. With a conceptual and ethical anchorage, educators can avoid jumping on questionable educational bandwagons while incorporating positive aspects of like-minded approaches.

They can also evaluate texts on Invitational Education and work on collaborative efforts to modify the theory. The International Alliance for Invitational Education provides an international forum for discussing both theory and practice. At this step, practitioners of Invitational Education can explain it in multiple ways to varied audiences. (A key test to check on this ability is to explain Invitational Education without using the word "inviting.")

Confrontation of Major Issues (Step 11)

Advanced understanding of Invitational Education can begin with reflective insight, but it culminates in creative application. Participants in this step of the HELIX can take a proactive stance toward challenges that are facing their school, their community, and the larger society. Thus, they can address, in a civil way, basic issues regarding the symbolic webbing of their school. They ask and honestly seek answers to such questions as these:

- Are we really who we say we are?
- What is the "elephant in the room" that we are not addressing?
- Are there some students in our school who are being left out?
- Are there some issues or policies in the larger community or society that work against our students?
- How are we preparing students to be caring participants in a democratic society?

Developing answers to these questions leads to creating more inviting school practices and a socially integrating sense of purpose. An important process here is to use student, parent, and community insights and participation to develop a deep sense of purpose for the school.

Transformation (Step 12)

By this step, invitational theory is rooted in every aspect of life in and around the school. It is reflected in people's interactions, the school's outside and inside appearance, the programs established, the policies supported, and the processes that are followed. The school acts as an inviting family in that it consistently demonstrates respect for individual uniqueness, cooperative spirit, sense of belonging, pleasing habitat, positive expectations, and vital connections to society.

In the spirit of transformation, staff members are able to articulate where they started, where they are now, and the framework and processes used to get there. Individuals and school teams are asked to present programs at meetings and conferences to describe how and why their school works—and they do this with enthusiasm, grace, sincerity, and skill. Their school is seen as a model for what education can become. School community members have learned the creative merger of the possible and the imaginative in handling conflict and in developing principled plans of action. Their school is filled with hope as they continually seek ways to put into practice the assumptions of Invitational Education:

- People are able, valuable, and responsible and should be treated accordingly.
- Education is a cooperative, collaborative process where everyone matters.
- The process is the product in the making.
- People possess relatively boundless potential in all areas of worthwhile human endeavor.

- Human potential can best be realized by places, policies, programs, and processes that are specifically designed to encourage human potential, and by people who are intentionally inviting with themselves and others, personally and professionally.

Invitational Education can have a positive, sustained, and creative impact on school cultures. The Invitational HELIX was developed with this in mind to guide spokespersons who have an awareness of the deep commitments involved in the theory; possess a sound and expanding understanding of its parts and whole; apply imaginatively and courageously its techniques and spirit; and use skill and persistence to develop within their schools an inviting culture and connections to a more democratic society. This requires deep commitments, solid thinking, and coordinated actions.

As Michael Fullan (1991) pointed out, the process of change is not usually some sequential, step-by-step approach. Many factors enter into the change equation and often, at best, it is two steps forward and one step back. The Invitational HELIX is not a magic formula that can change this; however, the HELIX can engender discussion and offer suggestions regarding future steps. Using the HELIX to start a dialogue about where a school should be going can be a way to get a school unstuck. The Invitational HELIX is based on hope for positive change. Creating inviting schools is fundamentally an imaginative act of hope, along with some systematic strategies.

Creating inviting schools is fundamentally an imaginative act of hope.

SUMMARY

This chapter offered the Invitational HELIX as a structured plan for creating and sustaining schools that are both safe and successful. The logical structure of the plan should be clear. The psychological implementation of the plan may be elusive, at first. Chapter 7 describes how change goes through four clear stages: Awareness, Understanding, Application, and Adoption. The HELIX builds on these four stages in creating, sustaining, and enhancing truly caring and welcoming schools.

Moving from occasional interest to systematic application to pervasive adoption, the HELIX shows how a school can more deeply embody an inviting perspective. We now move on to how this approach is being applied in schools around the world.

GETTING STARTED

1. What would make *your* experience at school better? During the Structured Dialogue (Step 2 of the HELIX), staff members may be asked to work in small groups to identify two things they really enjoy experiencing at their school, as well as two things they would like to change that would improve their experience and be fairly easy to accomplish. This exercise helps the staff to identify and address their needs first.

   Seated in groups of 4–6 people, staff members write their two ideas on a piece of large chart paper. A representative from each group posts their group's chart on a wall and explains their ideas. The ideas are simply presented but not discussed. When all ideas have been posted, each staff member is given three small stickers and is invited to put their stickers on the ideas that they feel are easy to address and most important to them. They may choose to put more than one of their stickers on a single item. When all staff members have placed their stickers on the charts, it will become apparent where the school might begin to improve the school's climate. Volunteers are then asked to work together to address the top concerns. Exercises like this help to move the staff from theory to practice and generate buy-in for school improvement efforts.

2. Invitational Education asks all stakeholders to reflect on their choice of words and actions. During Step 4 of the HELIX, encourage staff members to try an invitational approach in their communication with students, parents, and staff. This typically leads to some surprisingly successful encounters and resolutions. Allow a few minutes at the beginning of every faculty, team, and administrative meeting to share these success stories.

3. As the staff begins to experience the benefits of an invitational framework for positive school climate, it is important to formally organize the efforts of volunteers into committees identified by the 5 Ps (People, Places, Policies, Programs, and Processes). Time should be set aside for committee leaders to meet together with building leaders on a regular basis. When staff members are willing to devote time to making the school a more socially and emotionally safe place, their efforts need to become a priority in the school. Regular meetings and reports back to the full staff demonstrate support for the initiatives. Invitational committees should never become elite groups. Encourage naysayers to express their concerns and leave the door open for anyone to join a discussion or project.

CHAPTER 8

Invitational Education at Work

Thousands of candles can be lighted from a single candle
And the life of the candle will not be shortened.

—Siddhartha Gautama (The Buddha)

Hundreds of schools around the globe have used Invitational Education to create and sustain socially and emotionally safe places for teaching and learning. With an invitational framework at the core of their mindsets, messages, and actions, these schools are enjoying positive changes in both school climate and academic achievement. Here are some highlights about what just a few of our inviting schools have experienced and accomplished. Feel free to reach out to the school leaders for more information about their journey and initiatives. As you consider using an invitational framework for your school improvement efforts, remember that it can begin with a single individual and classroom, and grow to include all stakeholders in a building, district, or geographic region.

DISTRICTWIDE INITIATIVES

Most districtwide invitational initiatives start in a single school with educators who begin learning about and modeling Invitational Education. Success comes from acknowledging the strengths and contributions of all stakeholders and continuing to invite their participation throughout the journey. Leaving the door open and learning from naysayers' perspectives builds a respectful and optimistic environment for change.

Carlsbad Schools, New Mexico

Imagine a school that has been through five principals in 7 years. Imagine that at this same school substitute teachers did not want to come back. Imagine that also in this school only 41% of students were making 85% or above on Accelerated Reader tests. Now imagine that this school received a grade of "D" from the state Education Department, only three points removed from an "F." It is not hard to imagine that members of this school were frustrated and perplexed. Hope seemed a remote possibility.

Now imagine this school with a new principal, who came in with energy, commitment, and a vision that teachers, staff, parents, and students embraced and extended. Imagine that now, in this same school, substitute teachers seek to work there but usually do not get a chance because teachers are seldom absent. Imagine that this school moved from a grade of "D" to a "B" (the highest grade that was given in the system) and the number of students making 85% or better on Accelerated Reader tests went up from 41% to 90%. Now imagine also that a 2nd-grade teacher just won Teacher of the Year in the state, the principal won Principal of the Year, and the school received the Program of the Year award. In 2017, the school was one of only two in New Mexico to receive the National Distinguished Title I School award. This certainly sounds like a stretching of the imagination, but it really happened at Joe Stanley Smith Elementary School in Carlsbad, New Mexico, a great place to learn and visit.

Joe Stanley Smith's principal, Kim Arrington, went on to become the Carlsbad Municipal School District's director of elementary education. Inspired by the "change in chemistry" at just one school, Invitational Education is now being implemented in several of the Carlsbad schools, with each building creating its own path and set of initiatives.

Of special note is the new Carlsbad Early College High School, established in 2014, which developed out of a successful partnership with New Mexico State University Carlsbad, Carlsbad Municipal Schools, and the local business community. An invitational framework underscores this unique approach to offering students both high school and college credit, while pursuing a program of study that prepares them for higher education and workforce opportunities in southeastern New Mexico. In 2018, Carlsbad Early College High School had a 95% graduation rate and was recognized by *U.S. News & World Report* as one of America's best high schools. The school was ranked 27th in the state of New Mexico.

Students at all different levels of academic achievement may apply to attend the Early College program for 4 years. In an accelerated program, they earn a state-recognized high school diploma during the first 2 years, and an associate degree or 2 years of college credit during the last 2 years, which includes internships in their areas of interest. Students are well prepared to then enter the workforce or continue on to complete a baccalaureate degree.

Early College High School provides 2 years of college at no cost to the student, as it is part of their high school experience. Many of the students represent the first generation in their family to attend college, and they would not have had the encouragement and financial means to do so without this opportunity. Carlsbad's Early College High School is a great example of how student, school, community, and workforce needs can be met when all students are seen as able, valuable, and responsible and their learning is connected to their interests.

Jessamine County Schools, Kentucky

The Jessamine County School District's invitational journey provides compelling insights at various levels in the Nicholasville, Kentucky, school system—from districtwide adoption, to classroom and school implementations, and perhaps most important, a personal student story. Jessamine County is a suburban school district with 10 traditional schools, an alternative secondary school, and a secondary career and technology center. The student population is 82% White and 56.6% of the students receive free or reduced lunch. Of the 10 traditional schools, seven have applied for and received international Inviting School Awards and the career and technology center is currently beginning their invitational journey.

All are enjoying benefits from their commitment to sustaining an invitational framework for all academic, social, and emotional initiatives. The district had a 94.5% attendance rate for the 2016–2017 school year. Many schools received distinguished academic ratings that year. In 2018, both Jessamine County high schools had a 96% graduation rate. The district's commitment to being personally and professionally inviting to its students, staff, and community has led to nine student exchange programs with elementary and secondary students in Hong Kong, and four teacher exchanges with schools in Hong Kong and mainland China. Invitational Education has provided many global learning opportunities for a community that is not significantly diverse. Participating staff and families have shared inspiring stories about what these cultural exchanges have meant to them.

Much can be learned from the journey of the newest building in the district, the Red Oak Elementary School, which opened in the fall of 2013. Principal Andrea McNeal and the District's IE Coordinator and 2nd-grade teacher Angela Miller led the development of the new school's shared mindset and practices, intentionally built upon an invitational framework. The importance of relationships and communication was stressed in every aspect of the school. Staff, students, and parents were invited to join the 5-P committees right from the start. Red Oak received students from five existing elementary schools, so they were able to track student progress and note growth during the students' Red Oak years. In 2013–2014, the new school's academic scores ranked last in the county. However, by 2015–2016, Red Oak was ranked highest in the district, and received a "School of Distinction/High Progress School" rating from the state.

Unique instructional strategies that helped students take charge of their own learning are evident in all classrooms. For example, parent-teacher conferences are led by the elementary students, who monitor their own progress throughout the semester and explain their strengths and areas in need of improvement to their parents. Students help to develop classroom routines in a "doing with" approach to creating a safe environment. Substitute teachers marvel at how these young students take charge of procedures and transitions even when their teacher is not present.

School success begins with the individual student. When Red Oak Elementary opened its doors, it received many students who had been labeled as "problem" students by their previous schools. The Red Oak staff decided early on that they would not label students, but instead get to know the students and what made them thrive or shut down. For example, Dee lived in a dysfunctional household, and by the time she arrived at Red Oak she had missed 35% of the prior school year due to truancy. Dee often cursed, threw tantrums, and ran through the hallways, yelling or throwing things. In response to things that others said and did, she would often blurt out inappropriate comments and roll her eyes. Despite her behavior, the staff embraced her with loving kindness and Dee's tough exterior began to soften.

Dee's attendance began to improve, as did her attitude, choices of behavior, and work ethic. While at Red Oak, she disliked vacation weeks for she looked forward to being at school. One day she called the principal to ask for someone to pick her up because her mother had not put her on the bus that morning.

Dee became a successful student in every way. She was a leader in her grade, a school ambassador, and was chosen by her classmates to give the 5th-grade graduation speech. Dee made a successful transition to middle school, where she maintains good grades, high attendance, and has earned awards running track.

Jessamine County's success in implementing and sustaining an invitational framework was greatly aided by steadfast and consistent support from the district administration, led by then Superintendent Kathy Fields and school building leaders, who believed that dedicating time and resources to improving school climate would reap academic benefits.

Scott County Schools, Kentucky

The role of school leaders in changing school climate cannot be underestimated. Jessamine County's school leaders were inspired by Scott County Schools, a nearby district of 14 schools that embedded the invitational framework into the fabric of every school and classroom. Scott County's central office not only trained every employee in the entire district on invitational theory and practice and hosted an international IAIE conference; they partnered with the Toyota Corporation of Kentucky and successfully blended Toyota's Quality Training Principles with Invitational Education. Scott County enjoys a strong community partnership with the Toyota Corporation and other businesses in Scott County, often training new teachers along with new Toyota employees. The Board of Education adopted 14 Principles based on Invitational Education and Toyota's Quality Training, which serve as guiding statements for every decision made in the district.

REGIONAL INITIATIVES IN NEW YORK

Can a single teacher serve as the catalyst for creating an inviting school? In New York State, all Long Island educators are invited to attend regional workshops on school climate strategies, sponsored by the Long Island Social Emotional Literacy Forum (LI SELF.) This volunteer group of educators collaborates with local government education agencies to provide school climate workshops at little or no charge, open to any staff member from the 120 Long Island school districts and all of New York City Schools.

Recently, New York State became the first state to mandate mental health education, pre-K through Grade 12. All school districts in New York are now learning how to integrate sequential social and emotional learning lessons in all grades, as well as striving to improve school climate.

As the mental health mandate unfolds, school leaders and their school climate committees are often overwhelmed by the vast array of programs that promise to improve school climate, student behavior, and academic achievement. Whether it is social–emotional learning lessons, trauma-informed school techniques, restorative practices, or a growth-mindset program, these valuable initiatives often fail to realize their goals because the communication skills of every school adult are not considered or developed. Countless school climate initiatives lose steam and get shelved because the influence and skills of school adults are ignored.

Invitational Education is providing a much-needed framework to support, integrate, and sustain these "Tier I" (for all students) interventions. An invitational framework is effective because it concentrates on developing the communication skills of all school adults and inviting practices in all domains of the school. Other initiatives often involve just the teachers who are going to deliver the social–emotional learning lesson or lead a restorative conflict resolution session. When schools start with Invitational Education, every adult the students interact with is learning how to intentionally message colleagues, students, and parents with care, optimism, respect, and trust. This lays a foundation upon which other school climate initiatives can flourish.

Many schools in the Long Island area have chosen to use an invitational framework for their school climate work and now serve as model schools. Regional workshops provide an opportunity for individuals not only to learn new strategies, but to network with other like-minded professionals, share ideas, visit schools, and provide feedback to the NY State Education Department. Often just one teacher or school leader happens to attend a regional IE workshop and brings the invitational framework back to their school, planting the seed for school transformation.

Rocky Point Middle School, Rocky Point, NY

Inviting schools on Long Island run the gamut from high-achieving, high-socioeconomic schools to high-poverty schools that have many social and academic challenges. Entering their hallways and classrooms, one would not be able to tell them apart. Rocky Point Middle School used Invitational Education to survey what students wanted and needed most from their school. They significantly broadened the choices available for clubs and things to do during lunch recess. A game room created for students out of a storage closet led to positive interactions between students of different grade levels. Building on the power of positive relationships and communication, Rocky Point recently created an advisory program during which staff members meet bimonthly with a group of 12 students to develop team-building skills and discuss issues important to adolescents.

While interviewing a large group of students at Rocky Point, one of the authors noted that every single student was able to name a strength or talent that they possessed, which had been pointed out to them by a staff member. Many reported that the staff member had also suggested or provided a way for them to further develop their talent. Staff members credit Principal Scott O'Brien for modeling invitational leadership. Many reported that whenever they propose a new program or request new resources, Dr. O'Brien supports their interest enthusiastically and finds a way to make it happen. Today, Dr. O'Brien continues to lead positive-climate initiatives districtwide, as the superintendent of schools for the Rocky Point School District.

Woodland Middle School, East Meadow, NY

The Woodland Middle School in East Meadow, New York, had a longstanding Social Emotional Learning Committee, comprised of a small group of staff and students who implemented a variety of positive initiatives. When they introduced the faculty to Invitational Education, they asked every teacher, "If there was one thing that you could change in the school that would make *your* experience at Woodland better, what would it be?" The teachers wrote their wish on a starfish-shaped note card and placed it in one of five boxes labeled for the 5 Ps: People, Places, Policies, Programs, and Processes.

Assistant Principal Patricia Graham described what happened next as a "tidal wave" of new participation in school climate initiatives. As committee members worked on implementing the staff's requests, people began to see their wishes become reality, leading to many more staff members volunteering to help. The school's 5-P Committees are now bursting with new members and ideas. Relationships throughout the school have improved significantly as people work side by side to insure everyone feels valued. For this large school comprised of two separate academic houses, positive relationships and building-wide collaboration has become the new norm.

Woodland has implemented countless initiatives to acknowledge innovative projects and kind acts by both students and staff. Here are just a few:

- At every academic team meeting, the staff members now take time to discuss five different students, called "The Valuable Five," for their positive contributions, effort, and improvement. By the end of the year, every student will have been acknowledged. Also significant, the meetings always end on a positive note as teachers learn what is unique about their students.
- Students who study sign language meet weekly at a local McDonald's with their instructor to socialize and communicate with deaf students who attend their school or live in the community.
- Students identified as needing help with social skills are invited to have lunch with volunteer students who engage them in games and activities.
- The "Highlights" program fills the main lobby showcases with pictures and descriptions honoring staff as well as student initiatives.
- "Treasure Your Suggestions" is the name of a treasure box in which school and community members are encouraged to place their suggestions for enhancing their school's inviting atmosphere.
- In addition to every staff member reading *The Fundamentals of Invitational Education* (Purkey & Novak, 2016) and discussing it at department meetings, 100 student leaders were trained in the tenets of Invitational Education. They then led a reflective activity in their homeroom classes focusing on what it means to treat others as able, valuable, and responsible.

Woodland's accomplishments certainly underscore the benefit of acknowledging both staff and student needs and interests.

John W. Dodd Middle School, Freeport, NY

John W. Dodd Middle School in Freeport, New York, uses Invitational Education to embrace their groundbreaking work in teaching social–emotional learning skills and mindfulness practices to every student and staff member in the school. Each morning at Dodd Middle School begins with an 8-minute mindfulness breathing activity. Consciously breathing in different patterns engages the parasympathetic nervous system and counters the automatic flight or fight response that is often triggered by stressful experiences. These mindful exercises are supported by a 5-week social–emotional learning curriculum (taught in 7th-grade health classes) during which students learn safe ways to cope with stress. Principal Johane Ligonde (2016) explains, "Students have become empowered to take ownership of their emotions and responsibility for their actions. They practice being 'button-proof,' or retaining their power, rather than being receptacles for other people's taunts." By immersing this work in an invitational framework, students, staff, and parents have become more skillful in choosing words and actions that communicate their belief that everyone is able, valuable, and responsible. Thus, the number of negative triggers and responses has been drastically reduced.

The Dodd student population is highly diverse, with 70% of the students being eligible for free or reduced lunch, and 11% being English language learners. In response to high expectations for all, Dodd students are excelling academically, with many students involved in unique science and technology programs, taking and passing high school–level courses, and increasing scores on NY State assessments by 5–12 points. Discipline data from the 2015–2016 school year showed a decrease in the total number of infractions from 1,183 in the previous year to 716—the lowest amount in 6 years. In ongoing research at UCLA, the impact of Dodd's SEL program was studied, showing a statistically significant increase in attentional focus, a significant (12.7%) decrease in fear and anxiety, and a highly significant (18%) increase in self-efficacy. With words and actions firmly rooted in Invitational Education, Dodd Middle School is thriving.

Charles A. Mulligan Middle School, Central Islip, NY

Charles A. Mulligan Middle School in Central Islip received significant improvements in their state education evaluation report after implementing Invitational Education. Town meetings for each grade level to discuss school issues, and individual SMART goals developed by students and reviewed with staff members every quarter, are just some of the initiatives that help students see themselves as able, valuable, and responsible. (SMART goals are Specific, Measurable, Achievable, Realistic, and Timely.) The school requires students to earn community-service credits, which can be accomplished by participating in school activities, and in the many clubs available, and even by going to teachers for extra help, since improving their academic achievement is viewed as a positive contribution to the school community. Many staff members can be found at school throughout vacation weeks and summer months, providing opportunities for academic assistance, relationship building, and just a place to have breakfast and some fun. Mulligan went on to implement a comprehensive social–emotional learning curriculum with weekly student lessons and service-learning projects that involve the whole community.

Recently, due to a shift in enrollment, the Mulligan Middle School was transformed into an elementary intermediate school. While the 7th- and 8th-grade teachers, sadly, transferred to another building, the remaining 6th-grade and special-area teachers and Dr. Tracy Hudson, their resolute principal, embraced the change and continued their invitational initiatives with the new staff.

Schools around the world are inspiring others through their unique initiatives and their significant academic and behavioral gains achieved by developing school improvement projects within an invitational framework.

INTERNATIONAL APPLICATIONS

All around the world, well-nourished seeds of Invitational Education have transformed over 450 schools in Hong Kong, mainland China, Australia, Mexico, Canada, South Africa, Dominican Republic, Hungary, Malta, Singapore, the United Kingdom, and the United States of America. Invitational Education provides a universal language of transformation that appeals to a broad and diverse population worldwide.

Clarkson Community High School, Western Australia

Under the leadership of Principal John Young, the Clarkson Community High School, located in Perth, Western Australia, is using an invitational framework for their systemwide reform efforts, which include continuous reflective practice and data-driven instruction. Recognizing that systemwide improvements must flow through to the classroom, the Clarkson staff members put every child at the center of learning. As Principal Young explains,

> Many of the (grade 7–12) students entering the school as new
> enrollees, are achieving significantly below national minimum
> standards set by the Australian Curriculum Assessment and Reporting
> Authority. For example, in one year, the national benchmark standard
> for mean performance in most areas tested was approximately 540.
> Students entering Clarkson were 60 below the mean in reading, 73
> below in writing, 74 below in spelling, 46 below in numeracy, and 85
> below in grammar. (personal communication, April 11, 2020)

Clarkson's invitational, data-driven approach has produced significant gains in academic performance and positive behaviors. In reviewing suspension rates, Young reports that prior to implementing Invitational Education strategies, the 2009 suspension rate at Clarkson was 57%. By 2016, the suspension rate had dropped to 20% (personal communication, April 11, 2020). Steady improvements in course grades have also been noted as students become more engaged and connected to school.

Adam Inder is the head of learning for math and science at Clarkson. He is passionate about exploring how contemporary research such as Invitational Education and John Hattie's *Visible Learning* (2009) can help socioeconomically disadvantaged schools. Inder (2017, pp. 25–26) explains that "Clarkson Community High School is a school that is intentional in its decision making." The staff believes that "this is the driving factor behind consistently high achievements that appear to (in part) defy expectations of achievement in high-stakes testing." Inder has been tracking Clarkson's NAPLAN (Australia's literacy and numeracy assessment) results along with the change in the school's ICSEA (Index of Community Socio-Educational Advantage.) Looking at Grade 9 data from 2011 to 2016 "there has been a steady incline of NAPLAN results alongside a steady increase of ICSEA." However, in 2016 NAPLAN scores at Clarkson continued to climb, even though the ICSEA dropped. Inder notes, "This may suggest that Clarkson's NAPLAN scores are on an upward trend irrespective of the SES [socioeconomic status] of the school and its clientele" (p. 26). At Clarkson, poverty is not an excuse for failure.

Care, optimism, respect, and trust are evident to students and families from their first encounter with the school. A visit to the Clarkson Community High School website (http://www.clarksonchs.wa.edu.au) reveals a school where invitational practices are visible everywhere. For example, the Year 7 Transition Prospectus provides new students with a detailed explanation of the school's CARE program (Cooperation And Respect for Everyone). Students start their day in a meeting with their CARE teacher, who is that student's contact person for any concerns they might have or any social, emotional, or academic support they might need. Each CARE teacher collaborates with the Year Coordinator, organizing activities for students and overseeing student well-being. In addition, the school has chaplains and psychologists to provide counseling and advice. Indigenous students have additional support from Aboriginal and Islander Education Officer support staff.

Clarkson school leaders regularly publish articles in which they report and reflect on their invitational initiatives and academic success. These are available on the "Downloads" tab of the school's website, under "Published Articles." For example, *Learning Journey 3* (2018) documents the significant academic and behavioral improvements that occurred in recent years at Clarkson. Principal Young hopes their story will provide new insights and ideas for your own school climate journey.

The Hong Kong and Mainland China IE Initiatives

To date, 125 kindergarten, primary, and secondary schools in Hong Kong and 40 schools in the cities of Canton, Nanjing, Changchun, and Macau in mainland China have implemented Invitational Education with a steadfast commitment to creating more humane schools. Nowhere in the world has the pressure of high-stakes testing and competition been greater—for centuries. Dr. Peter Wong, retired chief curriculum officer for the Education Bureau in Hong Kong, has led the Invitational Education initiative for 18 years. Beginning with a pilot project for nine schools, professional development training, continuous coaching support, and opportunities to share invitational strategies and successes have encouraged many Hong Kong schools to pursue their invitational journey for many years. They thrive on discovering new ways to improve all aspects of their schools.

With the establishment of the IAIE Hong Kong Center and regional training, educators have broadened their knowledge of and commitment to the social and emotional health of students, staff, and parents. From the high academic performing Creative Secondary School to the Haven of Hope Sunny Side School for students with special needs, Hong Kong's IE schools have increased students' skills by implementing like-minded programs like social–emotional learning and mindfulness, as well as by exchanging instructional strategies with colleagues in the United States.

No visit to Hong Kong schools would be complete without a stop at the Creative Primary School, where Principal Clio Chan credits the remarkable success of their school to the community's commitment to nurturing all staff to become educational leaders. More than 25% of the school's staff have traveled halfway around the world to attend the International Alliance for Invitational Education's Annual World Conference and to visit schools in many nations. Principal Chan believes that establishing an invitational framework has helped the school to successfully meet all challenges, including the demands of designing new curricula and assessments to meet 168 standards of practice to become an International Baccalaureate school.

At the core of Creative Primary School's social, emotional, and academic success is the invitational commitment to helping all students realize their potential. Whether a child is performing like a professional on the piano, reading a 600-page book at lightning speed, leading an international service-learning project, or creating an original finger puppet show or a simple kite, all students are celebrated for their individual interests and accomplishments. This is indeed Invitational Education in action.

Creative Primary School received the IAIE Inviting School Award in 2002 and five additional IAIE Fidelity School Awards, culminating with the Gold Fidelity Award in 2015. Eighteen years later, IE remains well embedded in the school's culture, system, and policies. Principal Clio Chan's inspiring, detailed account of Creative Primary School's inviting programs, policies, and practices are described in more detail in *Creating Inviting Schools* (Novak et al., 2006).

The IAIE Hong Kong Center has made great strides in sharing invitational practices with schools in mainland China. Upon entering the Nanjing No. 54 Middle School campus, visitors are mesmerized by a beautifully landscaped, tranquil environment with gentle fountains and peaceful places to read and learn. With a new emphasis on the experience and process of learning and not just the final product, students confidently demonstrate where they are in the process, even when a skill has not yet been perfected.

Nanjing No. 54 Middle School teachers are encouraged to develop their personal talents, interests, and expertise into new elective courses for students. The educators express delight in being able to choose a unique interest and share their passion with students. They explain that through Invitational Education practices, they are no longer singularly focused on grades, but, instead, are also considering their students' development and interests. This new emphasis on process rather than product still produces excellent academic results.

Asian IE schools are making significant strides in academic achievement as well as in the social and emotional welfare of all stakeholders. Hong Kong and mainland China educators are regular attendees at the International Alliance for Invitational Education (IAIE) Annual World Conference and are always interested in planning exchange programs with U.S. students and educators. Visit the IAIE website at www.invitationaleducation.org for more information about IAIE's International Exchange Program and the Annual World Conference.

INVITATIONAL EDUCATION BEYOND PRE-K–12 SCHOOLS

Invitational Education has positively influenced all types of organizations, from health-care agencies, to counseling centers, businesses, and universities. Every organization involves people, relationships, and communication. Whether employees, customers, or community members, everyone benefits from an invitational environment dedicated to helping them realize their full potential. What follow are a few of our university stories.

Muskingum University in New Concord, Ohio, is an intentionally inviting place. The Education Department began to label its approach as "invitational" in 2007, under the leadership of then Chair Vicki Wilson and Longaberger Chair for Teaching and Learning, Barb Hansen. All MU Education Department faculty receive a copy of *Fundamentals of Invitational Education* and model Invitational Education tenets in their communication with students and each other. An inviting approach is infused in all teaching, advising, and recruiting and in continued support after graduation.

Muskingum shares the invitational framework with their K–12 partner schools, providing professional development and involving staff in research projects. Their 10-year partnership with the Park Street Intermediate School in Columbus, Ohio, led to yearly exchange programs with Hong Kong schools and the establishment of the first IAIE state chapter in Ohio. (Other chapters have been established in Kentucky, West Virginia, New York, and New Mexico.)

Invitational Education is formally introduced to MU baccalaureate teacher candidates during their senior-year clinical experience. For graduate students, MU created a Masters of Education core course titled Inclusive Invitational Education. Muskingum University supports educators worldwide through their many years of presentations, guidance, and leadership in the International Alliance for Invitational Education.

The University of Findlay (Ohio) College of Education received the Inviting School Award in 2016. Through the process of becoming an inviting school, they developed goals to create a system-wide difference in how their faculty, staff, students, and community feel. Their Inviting School Survey results noted dramatic improvements in all 5-P areas of Invitational Education. The college's mission is "to prepare caring, competent, reflective, and highly qualified professionals by demonstrating respect for others, trust in our faculty and teacher candidates, and education partners, and optimism about the future and human potential of our candidates."

Findlay undergraduate students are introduced to Invitational Education in their student teaching capstone seminar. At the master's level, IE is reinforced in a core class, Collaboration: Education and Community, which is required of all master's level students. At the doctoral level, all students take a core class called Inviting Environments to Facilitate the Affective Domain, using the book *Becoming an Invitational Leader* (Purkey & Siegel, 2013). Two Findlay graduates have received IAIE Research awards for their outstanding work in invitational theory and practice. While striving to provide an invitational environment for their students and staff, Muskingum University and the University of Findlay have also demonstrated the importance of introducing Invitational Education to future educators.

These school stories represent just a few of the thriving schools that have created socially and emotionally safe environments through Invitational Education. Within the Invitational Education framework, school transformation is seen as an ongoing and often fragile process. Though the outcomes of this process are measurable, the changes that matter most are often intangible. The authors' experiences at many inviting schools have helped them to understand more about these intangibles. The changes that have mattered most are those that affect how teachers and students see themselves, each other, and their schools. As students and teachers develop more positive views, the momentum of Invitational Education grows, and the underlying structures that shape school cultures begin to change. Over time, schools become less like factories and more like families, where people want to spend their time and where everyone is summoned cordially to realize their relatively boundless potential in all areas of worthwhile human endeavor.

CONCLUSION

This book has explored the process of creating a more humane school climate through the intentional use of Invitational Education. By focusing on the subtle but pervasive messages extended in the school environment, *Developing Inviting Schools* has emphasized something familiar that has heretofore been overlooked. "The road to the City of Emeralds is paved with yellow brick," said the witch in *The Wizard of Oz*, "so you cannot miss it." But emerald cities, like invitations in schools, can sometimes be too obvious to see.

Four unhappy characters went to find the Wizard of Oz: a scarecrow who thought he had no brain, a tin woodsman who thought he had no heart, a lion who believed he had no courage, and a young girl who thought she lacked the power to make changes in her life. All were under the delusion that if they could only reach the Great and Powerful Oz, he would grant them the things they lacked. Little did they realize that they already possessed the very things they sought. When the four finally accomplished what they believed they could never do, they returned to the Emerald City impatient for their rewards. There they discovered that wizards (like educators) have no magic power.

Yet, the wizard did manage to do things "that everybody knows can't be done." He cared about people, and to each of the four he sent a most powerful invitation: "A testimonial! A decree!" He invited them to see things in themselves that they had overlooked and to use what they already possessed. The lion represents respect, the scarecrow represents optimism, the tinman represents trust, and Dorothy represents intentionality. As Dorothy said when she finally got back to Kansas: "Oh, Aunty Em, I've been to many strange and marvelous places looking for something that was right here all along . . . right in my own backyard!"

So it is with developing inviting schools.

Invitational Education Websites

THE INTERNATIONAL ALLIANCE FOR INVITATIONAL EDUCATION®

Promoting Positive Climates for Learning, Leading, and Living

The International Alliance for Invitational Education® (IAIE) is a not-for-profit, worldwide organization of educators and allied professionals who are dedicated to creating, sustaining, and enhancing positive environments that cordially summon people to realize their full potential.

Over 450 schools around the world have implemented a positive climate framework built on Invitational Theory and Practice and have received the IAIE Inviting School Award and Fidelity School Award. Inviting schools enjoy increased academic achievement, graduation and attendance rates, collaboration, engagement, and cooperation, while decreasing behavior problems, conflicts, suspensions, failures, and teacher burnout.

IAIE also serves as a network for organizations to share ideas globally. The Inviting School Survey-Revised provides an online tool through which school leaders can receive disaggregated data about their school climate, compared with similar schools around the world. IAIE also hosts an annual World Conference.

Membership in IAIE provides access to online member resources, including the *Journal of Invitational Theory and Practice*. More information about IAIE resources, programs, conferences, and membership is available at https://www.invitationaleducation.org

IAIE's Inviting School and Fidelity School Awards

IAIE provides schools with the opportunity to receive international awards, in recognition of the development of an intentionally positive climate based on the Invitational Education framework.

Schools new to positive climate initiatives as well as those that have been working on such initiatives for many years benefit greatly by participating in the Inviting School Award program. Invitational Education strategies provide a boost in staff morale, reflective practice, and renewed interest in school improvement that school leaders have described as a "tidal wave" of positive, renewed engagement.

The Inviting School Award is the first award for schools that have introduced Invitational Education to their staff and begun the process of implementing changes in the five domains of Invitational Education: People, Places, Policies, Programs, and Processes. Schools that receive the Inviting School Award are eligible to receive a series of five Fidelity Awards for their continued work in school improvement. Details about the awards programs may be found at: https://www.invitationaleducation.org/awards/

THE IAIE HONG KONG CENTER

The IAIE Hong Kong Center is responsible for significant growth in Inviting School practices in Hong Kong, mainland China, Thailand, and Singapore. One hundred sixty-five Asian Schools have achieved multiple Inviting and Fidelity School Awards through the guidance of the IAIE HK Center.

The Center provides comprehensive training for Asian schools interested in Invitational Education, bringing world-renown experts on school climate, leadership, and instructional practices to China.

The Center works closely with IAIE on all IAIE initiatives, especially the Inviting and Fidelity School Awards programs, the World Conference and Student Exchange Programs with U.S. schools. IAIE HK welcomes opportunities for student and educator exchange experiences. More information about IAIE Hong Kong Exchange Programs may be found at: https://www.invitationaleducation.org/student-exchange-program/

THE INVITATIONAL ONLINE TEACHER SURVEY

When working in a traditional classroom setting, teachers are better able to use nonverbal cues to convey invitations to students, as well as interpret a student's feelings and needs. Online instructors are often limited to written communication and possibly interactions through video. The way that an instructor communicates with students during online instruction can enhance or hinder learning.

The Invitational Online Teacher Assessment (Lockwood et al., 2014) is a free web-based instrument designed to be administered to students. It automatically scores the results and sends a report to the instructor via email. Located at www.nvitationalEdOnline.com, the website also includes a general overview of Invitational Education and a user manual for the IOTA.

The Inviting School Survey-Revised (ISS-R)

The Inviting School Survey-Revised (ISS-R) is a 50-item school climate survey to be completed online by students, teachers, school staff, and parents or guardians. The survey is designed to measure the degree to which schools summon people to realize their relatively boundless potential in five basic dimensions: People, Places, Policies, Programs, and Processes. It is available in English, Spanish, Traditional Chinese, and Simplified Chinese. A copy of the ISS-R questions follows this introduction.

Uses

1. To learn how students, teachers, administrators, staff, and parents perceive the school.
2. To identify areas of weakness and strength in the school climate.
3. To use as pre–post measures in assessing school improvement.
4. To identify schools that are eligible to receive the Inviting School Award or the Fidelity School Award.
5. To obtain scores on five factors plus a composite (total) score.
6. To compare your schools with others in our global community.

How to Access the Survey

The ISS-R online survey is available at https://www.invitationaleducation. org/resources/ You may complete the survey individually for free, by becoming a registered user on the site. You may also download a PDF copy. If you would like to have your organization's surveys collected, the data disaggregated, and receive a report on the findings, become an Organizational Member of IAIE and then go to the "Store" tab on the website to purchase the service for a nominal fee.

Collecting Responses and Scoring

A minimum of 100 survey responses should be collected; however, there is no limit to the number of responses you may submit. It is strongly suggested that a representative sample group be obtained. Ideally, the sample would survey 30% of the students, 30% of the teachers, 30% of the parents, and 10% of the school staff (e.g., administrators, counselors, and support staff). The °ISS-R (2016) is designed for online self-administration. Members of a school community or participants in a research study take the ISS-R individually, and their results are compiled for their assigned school or group. Most respondents complete the survey within 20 minutes. Scores for schools or other groups are compiled in spreadsheets. Each participating school/district will receive a detailed report.

International Alliance for
Invitational Education

Inviting School Survey - Revised (ISS-R)

*Thank you for your participation in this activity. It is very much appreciated! We are interested in your opinions on a range of issues regarding your school. Individual responses will be **strictly** confidential as aggregated data is only being analyzed school.*

1. Name of your school: _____

2. Are you: ☐ Male   ☐ Female

3. Are you a: ☐ Student   ☐ Teacher   ☐ Administrator
             ☐ Parent   ☐ Counselor   ☐ Other _____

4. If you are a student how old are you: _____

DIRECTIONS

The purpose of this survey is to determine what you think your school.   Following are a series of 50 statements concerning your school.   Please use the five-point response scale and select how much you agree or disagree for each item.   It should take approximately 15-20 minutes to complete.

SA=*Strongly Agree*   **A**=*Agree*   **U**=*Undecided*   **D**=*Disagree*   **SD**=*Strongly Disagree*
Select '**N/A**' only if the question does not apply to your school

	Statements	SA	A	U	D	SD	N/A
1	Student discipline is approached from a positive standpoint.						
2	Everyone is encouraged to participate in athletic (sports) programs.						
3	The principal involves everyone in the decision-making process.						
4	Furniture is pleasant and comfortable.						
5	Teachers are willing to help students who have special problems.						
6	Teachers in this school show respect for students.						
7	Grades are assigned by means of fair and comprehensive assessment of work and effort.						
8	The air smells fresh in this school.						
9	Teachers are easy to talk with.						
10	There is a wellness (health) program in this school.						
11	Students have the opportunity to talk to one another during class activities.						
12	Teachers take the time to talk with students about students' out-of-class activities.						
13	The school grounds are clean and well maintained.						
14	All telephone calls to this school are answered promptly and politely.						
15	Teachers are generally prepared for class.						
16	The restrooms in this school are clean and properly maintained.						
17	School programs involve out of school experience.						
18	Teachers exhibit a sense of humor.						
19	School policy encourages freedom of expression by everyone.						
20	The Principal's office is attractive.						
21	People in this school are polite to one another.						
22	Everyone arrives on time for school.						
23	Good health practices are encouraged in this school.						
24	Teachers work to encourage students' self-confidence.						
25	Bulletin boards are attractive and up-to-date.						

	Statements	SA	A	U	D	SD	N/A
26	The messages and notes sent home are positive.						
27	The Principal treats people as though they are responsible.						
28	Space is available for student independent study.						
29	People often feel welcome when they enter the school.						
30	Students work cooperatively with each other.						
31	Interruptions to classroom academic activities are kept to a minimum.						
32	Fire alarm instructions are well posted and seem reasonable.						
33	People in this school want to be here.						
34	A high percentage of students pass in this school.						
35	Many people in this school are involved in making decisions.						
36	People in this school try to stop vandalism when they see it happening.						
37	Classrooms offer a variety of furniture arrangements.						
38	The school sponsors extracurricular activities apart from sports.						
39	Teachers appear to enjoy life.						
40	Clocks and water fountains are in good repair.						
41	School buses wait for late students.						
42	School pride is evident among students.						
43	Daily attendance by students and staff is high.						
44	There are comfortable chairs for visitors.						
45	Teachers share out-of-class experiences with students.						
46	Mini courses are available to students.						
47	The grading practices in this school are fair.						
48	Teachers spend time after school with those who need extra help.						
49	The lighting in this school is more than adequate.						
50	Classes get started quickly.						

The Invitational Education Toolkit Professional Development Series

The Invitational Education Toolkit delivers a self-guided journey for any school planning to build greater school success. Rather than clone school improvement with a prescribed set of strategies, the Toolkit builds on the unique traits of each school, wherever its journey begins.

Twelve training steps lead schools along a continuum of invitational growth and development. Each progressive step starts with an intentionally designed PowerPoint lesson for stakeholders. Resources include detailed facilitator notes, engaging video clips, printable handouts, training tips, and collaboration opportunities for participants. Facilitators do not need in-depth experience with Invitational Education to lead the workshops.

Great flexibility is a hallmark of the Invitational Education Toolkit. PowerPoint lessons are designed for a 1-hour workshop. Lessons may be shortened, extended, or eliminated to match the school's situation. Each step prompts new thoughts and actions that continue to transform a school over days, weeks, and months.

The Invitational Education Toolkit is designed to support educators, from novices to experts. Every school stakeholder will benefit by applying Invitational Education steps, including service staff, counselors, health providers, parents, and students, as well as teachers and administrators. Schools applying for the Inviting School and Fidelity School Awards are encouraged to use the Toolkit to guide their journey. Information about pricing is available on the "Store" tab of the IAIE website. In addition, a free introductory PowerPoint is available on the IAIE website at https://www.invitationaleducation.org/product/invitational-education-toolkit/.

Research on Invitational Education

The International Alliance for Invitational Education (IAIE) maintains an up-to-date, comprehensive list of annotated references developed and maintained by Dr. Jenny Edwards of Fielding Graduate University. The list includes:

- 223 dissertations, masters theses, and presentations at conferences before 1991
- 214 articles since 1991
- 63 dissertations and masters theses since 1991
- 58 books and book chapters since 1991

Individuals undertaking research in Invitational Education may apply for the *IAIE Outstanding Research and Dissertation Awards*. The awards are presented annually to promote the scholarly study of the theory and practice of Invitational Education and to broaden and deepen its supportive research base. Applications may be submitted in the fall of each year by anyone who has completed research in the field of Invitational Education since June 30 of that same year. The research can be for a dissertation, or the research can be done independently.

Criteria

- Research is based on the theory and practice of Invitational Education
- Research contributes to the field of Invitational Education
- The study is of exemplary quality
- Nominees must be members of IAIE

For more information about the research awards and the latest edition of the IAIE Abstracts, please contact Dr. Jenny Edwards at jedwards@fielding.edu.

Researching an Evolving Theory of Practice

Working within an inviting framework provides many ways to think about, put into effect, and evaluate personal and professional educational practices. With this in mind, here is a framework for improving inviting theory, practice, and research.

Theory in Invitational Education deals with the working concepts and values that point in a democratic, perceptual, and self-concept direction. These general concepts need to be interpreted for specific situations. Doing this interpretive translation means everyone working from an inviting perspective has an evolving theory of practice.

Practice, the next step, means putting into action plans derived from or inspired by invitational theory or example. Because no two situations are the same, invitational theory needs to be interpreted differently in different places, and practices will need creative, on-the-spot adjustments, while still respecting the commitment to democratic, perceptual, and self-concept values.

Research comes in when looking at what was done and what needs to be accepted, modified, or held in abeyance in theory and practice as a result of what was found. Using this model, all who intentionally try an inviting perspective are simultaneously theoreticians, practitioners, and researchers. Theoreticians, because they are thinking with, critiquing, and adjusting the meaning and coherence of the key ideas and values of the approach. Practitioners, because some of their thinking is actually put into action and adjusted accordingly. Researchers, because they are examining what happened as a result of their thinking and doing. From this perspective, questions that might be asked include:

- What actually happened, from an inviting perspective?
- In what ways was this surprising?
- What changes did I make on the spot? Why?
- Upon reflection, what changes would I make next time?
- How has this experience made me different?
- How has my thinking about the inviting approach changed?
- How might I communicate this change in my approach to others?

Arranging a symposium with others who have tried this theory of practice research model can be a robust way of thinking about, doing, and studying the professional and personal commitments and dynamics for developing inviting schools.

An Introduction to the Metaphor of Blue and Orange Cards

William W. Purkey
December 2015

An imaginative way of thinking about Invitational Education is to imagine schools as dealing an endless supply of Blue Cards (beneficial) and Orange Cards (toxic). Everything in the school is a source of Blue and Orange Cards. Everything counts. Everything in the school can be measured by a single question. Will the people, places, policies, programs, and processes in this school be a source of Blue Cards or Orange ones?

The Blue and Orange Metaphor is a highly simplified explanation of Invitational Education's complexity. However, the metaphor does provide a sort of shorthand in visualizing and understanding the incredible power in inviting and disinviting school environments.

In Invitational Education everything matters. The ways the cans are stacked on the back loading dock, the ways the bathrooms smell, the ways phones are answered, the ways that people relate to one another, the ways that procedures, programs, and policies are created and followed. Everything in and around the school is inviting or disinviting. Nothing is neutral.

Each Blue or Orange Card sent and received varies in size and power. Some cards are so small as to be almost insignificant. Other cards are so large in impact that they can be a matter of life or death. Unfortunately, Orange Cards are far more powerful than Blue ones. As in life, it is easier to destroy than develop. The absence of Blue Cards in a school is tragic, but an even greater tragedy is a school of Orange Cards. To borrow from the medical profession, schools should first do no harm.

We give and receive myriad cards throughout our lives. These cards tell us who we are and how we fit into the world. Life is an endless quest for Blue Cards. If we are fortunate, our collection of Blue Cards is far greater than our collection of Orange ones. When there are too few Blue Cards, or too many Orange ones, people learn to question their own feelings and value and question the value of their relationships with others. The power of drugs and alcohol is that they often turn Orange Cards to Blue, but the effect is temporary. Simply stated, the best remedy for Orange Cards are lots of Blue ones, and the best preparation for Orange Cards is a storehouse of many Blue ones.

The process of collecting Blue and Orange Cards begins at birth, if not before. Children enter this world with absolute trust that adult caregivers will be the source of Blue Cards. They have absolute trust that they will be fed when hungry, cared for when hurt, comforted when fearful, and encouraged in their efforts to realize their relatively boundless potential in all areas of worthwhile human endeavor.

Even small children can grasp the significance of the cards. Once they learn the language of Blue and Orange Cards, it influences the way they think about things. They are quick to seek out Blue Cards, and to complain about Orange ones. Once the language has been explained and incorporated, students who feel mistreated or demeaned will say, "That's an Orange Card."

Orange Cards are a part of life. It is naïve to think that Orange Cards will vanish from human existence. However, schools do not need to increase the number. What schools can do is to invite the people who enter a school house door to view themselves as able, valuable, and responsible and to act accordingly. Each person in school should be encouraged to see the world as a good place to be, and that there are many things to love that will love them in return.

No amount of rationalizations or "special reasons" justifies Orange Cards. Whatever a hospital should be, it should not be a source of infection. Whatever a police department should be, it should not be a source of criminality. Whatever a government should be, it should not be a source of corruption. And whatever a school should be, it should not be a source of Orange Cards.

It is vital to remember that there are no discard piles in life. Every Blue Card and Orange Card you receive is forever. This being so, the metaphor is a constant reminder that schools should do everything they can to create, sustain, and enhance a truly Blue Card environment for everyone.

Purkey, W. W. (2015, December). *An introduction to the metaphor of blue and orange cards.* Retrieved July 11, 2020 at https://www.invitationaleducation.org/wp-content/uploads/2019/04/art_intro_metaphor_blue_orange_card-1.pdf. Reprinted with permission.

Note: The Blue and Orange Card Metaphor was first introduced in 1990 by William Purkey and Paula Stanley in *The Journal of Counseling and Development, May/June*(68), 587.

References

Adelman, H. S., & Taylor, L. (2014, January). *Bringing new prototypes into practice: Dissemination, implementation, and facilitating transformation* (Center Policy Brief). Center for Mental Health in Schools at UCLA.

Alberti, R. E., & Emmons, M. L. (1990). *Your perfect right: A guide to assertive living.* Impact.

Allport, G. W. (1955). *Becoming.* Yale University Press.

Allport, G. W. (1961). *Pattern and growth in personality.* Holt, Rinehart & Winston.

Ammerman, A., Smith, T. W., & Calancie, L. (2014). Practice-based evidence in public health: Improving reach, relevance, and results. *Annual Review of Public Health, 35,* 47–63.

Amos, W., & Purkey, W. W. (1988). Teacher practices and student satisfaction in dental hygiene programs. *Dental Hygiene, 62,* 286–291.

Anderson, W. T. (1990). *Reality isn't what it used to be: Theoretical politics, ready-to-wear religion, global myths, primitive chic, and other wonders of the postmodern world.* Harper.

Anglund, J. W. (1964). *A pocketful of proverbs.* Harcourt, Brace & World.

Arceneaux, C. J. (1994). Trust: An exploration of its nature and significance. *Journal of Invitational Theory and Practice, 3,* 35–49.

Arnold, W., & Roach, T. (1989) Teaching: A nonverbal communication event. *Business Education Forum, 44,* 18–20.

Astor, R. A., Bear, G. G., Bradshaw, C. P., Dewey, G. C., Espilage, D. L., Flannery, D., Furlong, M. J., Guerra, N., Jagers, R., Jimerson, S. R., Mayer, M. J., Nation, M., Nickerson, A. B., Noguera, P., Osher, D., Skiba, R., Sugai, G., Websyer, D. W., & Weist, M. D. (2018, February). *A call for action to prevent gun violence in the United States of America.* https://curry.virginia.edu/prevent-gun-violence

Bandura, A. (2012). Social cognitive theory. In P. A. M. Van Lange, A. W. Kruglanski, & E. T. Higgins (Eds.), *Handbook of theories of social psychology* (pp. 349–373). Sage Publications Ltd. https://doi.org/10.4135/9781446249215.n18

Bergman, K., & Gaitskill, T. (1990). Faculty and student perceptions of effective clinical teachers. *Journal of Professional Nursing, 6*(1), 33–44

Berliner, D. C., & Glass, G. V. (2014). *50 myths and lies that threaten America's public schools: The real crisis in education.* Teachers College Press.

Best High Schools in New Mexico (n.d.) U.S. News & World Report. Retrieved April 29, 2020, from https://www.usnews.com/education/best-high-schools /new-mexico/districts/carlsbad-municipal-schools/carlsbad-early-college-high -155523

Bidwell, A. (2014, August 21). *Duncan relaxes testing push, but teachers want more.* U.S. News & World Report. https://www.usnews.com/news/articles/2014/08/21 /education-secretary-arne-duncan-loosens-reins-on-teacher-evaluations-testing

Brady, K., Forton, M. B., & Porter, D. (2015). *Rules in school: Teaching discipline in the responsive classroom* (2nd ed.). Center for Responsive Teaching.

Branch, C., Damico, S., & Purkey, W. W. (1977). A comparison between the self-concepts-as-learner of disruptive and nondisruptive middle school students. *The Middle School Journal, 7,* 15–16.

Bregman, R. (2020). *Humankind: A hopeful history.* Bloomsbury Publishing.

Brown, C. (1965). *Manchild in the promised land.* Macmillan.

Buber, M. (1965). *The knowledge of man: Selected essays.* Harper & Row.

Butzin, S. M. (2018). *Creating joyful classrooms: A positive response to testing and accountability in the elementary school.* Roman & Littlefield.

Campbell, A. (2017, December 5). Making failure harder work than passing. *Edutopia.* https://www.edutopia.org/blog/making-failure-harder-work-angela-campbell

Canfield, J., & Wells, H. (1976). *100 ways to influence self-concept in the classroom: A handbook for teachers and parents.* Prentice Hall.

Cashman, J., Linehan, P., Purcell, L., Rosser, M., Schultz, S., & Skalski, S. (2014). *Leading by convening: A blueprint for authentic engagement.* National Association of State Directors of Special Education. http://www.ideapartnership.org /documents/NovUploads/Blueprint%20USB/NASDSE%20Leading%20by %20Convening%20Book.pdf

Centers for Disease Control and Prevention (2019). *Preventing adverse childhood experiences: Leveraging the best available evidence.* National Center for Injury Prevention and Control, Centers for Disease Control and Prevention. https:// www.cdc.gov/violenceprevention/pdf/preventingACES.pdf?deliveryName =USCDC_300-DM31480

Chapman, J. W. (1988). Learning disabled children's self-concept. *Review of Educational Research, 58,* 347–371.

Combs, A. W., Avila, D., & Purkey, W. W. (1978). *Helping Relationships: Basic Concepts for the Helping Professions* (2nd ed.). Pearson, Allyn & Bacon.

Combs, A. W., Soper, D. W., Gooding, C. T., Benton, J. A., Dickman, J. F., & Usher, R. H. (1969). *Florida Studies in the Helping Professions.* Social Science Monograph no. 37. University of Florida Press.

Coopersmith, S. (1967). *The antecedents of self-esteem.* W. H. Freeman.

Covington, M. V. (1984). The motive for self-worth. In R. A. Mes and C. Ames (Eds.). *Research in education: Student motivation* (pp. 77–113). Academic Press.

Csikszentmihalyi, M. (2014). *The collected works of Mihalyi Csikszentmihalyi.* Springer.

Damasio, A. (2018). *The strange order of things: Life, feeling, and the making of cultures*. Pantheon Books.

Deci, E. L. (1971). Effects of externally mediated rewards on intrinsic motivation. *Journal of Personality and Social Psychology, 18*(1), 105–115. https://doi .org/10.1037/h0030644

Deci, E. L. (with Flaste, R.). (1995). *Why we do what we do*. Penguin Books.

Deci, E. L., & Ryan, R. M. (1985). *Intrinsic motivation and self-determination in human behavior*. Plenum Press.

Deci, E. L., & Ryan, R. M. (1987). The support for autonomy and the control of behavior. *Journal of Personality and Social Psychology, 53*(6), 1024–1037.

Deci, E. L., & Ryan, R. M. (1991). A motivational approach to self: Integration in personality. In R. Dienstbier (Ed.), *Nebraska Symposium on Motivation: Vol. 38. Perspectives on motivation*, pp. 237–288). Plenum Press.

Deci, E. L., & Ryan, R. M. (2008). Facilitating optimal motivation and psychological well-being across life's domains. *Canadian Psychology, 49*(1), 14–23.

Deci, E. L., & Ryan, R. M. (2017). *Self-determination theory: Basic psychological needs in motivation, development and wellness*. Guilford Press.

Dewey, J. (1916/1966). *Democracy and education: An introduction to the philosophy of education*. Free Press/Macmillan.

Dewey, J. (1930). *Individualism old and new*. Minton, Balch & Company.

Dewey, J. (1933). *How we think: A restatement of the relation of reflective thinking to the educative process*. D. C. Heath.

Dweck, C. S. (2000). *Self-theories: Their role in motivation, personality and development*. Psychology Press.

Dweck, C. S. (2006). *Mindset: The new psychology of success*. Random House.

Edwards, J. (2010). *Inviting students to learn: 100 tips for talking effectively with your students*. ASCD.

Edelwich, J. (with Brodsky, A.). (1980). *Burnout: Stages of disillusionment in the helping professions*. Human Science Press.

Egan, G. (1990). *The skilled helper* (4th ed.). Brooks/Cole.

Esquivel, L. (1992). *Like water for chocolate*. Doubleday.

Fugua, D., Newman, J., Anderson, M., & Johnson, A. (1986). Preliminary study of internal dialogue in a training setting. *Psychological Reports, 58*, 163–172.

Gardner, H. (1991). *The unschooled mind: How children think and how schools should teach*. Basic Books.

Gardner, H. (1999). *The disciplined mind: Beyond facts and standardized tests, the K–12 education every child deserves*. Simon and Schuster.

Gardner, H. (2011). *Frames of mind: The theory of multiple intelligences*. Basic Books.

Goffin, S. G. (1989). How well do we respect the children in our care? *Childhood Education, 66*(2), 68–74. https://doi.org/10.1080/00094056.1989.10522487

Goldstein, D. (2014). *The teacher wars: A history of America's most embattled profession*. Penguin Random House.

Good, T. L., & Brophy, J. E. (1994). *Looking in classrooms* (6th ed.). HarperCollins College Publishers.

Gordon, T. (1974). *T.E.T.: Teacher-effectiveness training.* Peter H. Wyden.

Gregory, D. (1964). *Nigger.* Simon & Schuster.

Green, L. W. (2008, December 1). Making research relevant: If it is an evidence-based practice, where's the practice-based evidence? *Family Practice, 25*(1), i20–i24. https://doi.org/10.1093/fampra/cmn055

Greene, R. W. (2014). *Lost at School.* Simon & Schuster.

Haberman, M. (1995). *Star teachers of children in poverty.* Kappa Delta Pi.

Haberman, M. (1994). Gentle teaching in a violent society. *Educational Horizons, 72*(3), 131–135.

Harper, K. L., & Purkey, W. W. (1993). Self-concept-as-learner of middle level students. *Research in Middle Level Education, 17*(1), 79–89.

Harris, D., Warren, J., & Adler, C. (2017). *Meditation for fidgety skeptics: A 10% happier how-to book.* Spiegel & Grau.

Harter, S. (1983). Developmental perspectives on the self-system. In P. H. Mussen (Ed.), *Handbook of Child Psychology: Vol. 4* (pp. 275–385).

Harter, S. (1988). *Developmental processes in the construction of the self.* In T. D. Yawkey & J. E. Johnson (Eds.), *Integrative processes and socialization: Early to middle childhood* (pp. 45–78). Lawrence Erlbaum Associates.

Hattie, J. A. (1992). *Self-Concept.* Lawrence Erlbaum Associates.

Hattie, J. A. (2009). *Visible learning: A synthesis of over 800 meta-analyses relating to achievement.* Echo Point Books & Media.

Hattie, J. A. (2017). *Updated list of factors influencing student achievement.* https://visible-learning.org/wp-content/uploads/2018/03/VLPLUS-252-Influences-Hattie-ranking-DEC-2017.pdf

Hedegaard H., Warner M., & Miniño, A. M. (2017, December). *Drug overdose deaths in the United States,* 1999–2016 (NCHS Data Brief, no 294). National Center for Health Statistics.

Heward, W. L. (2012). *Exceptional children: An introduction to special education.* Pearson.

Hook, S. (1939). *John Dewey: An intellectual portrait.* John Day.

House, J. D. (1992). The relationship between perceived task competence, achievement expectations, and school withdrawal of academically underprepared adolescent students. *Child Study Journal, 22*(4), 253–272.

Howell, W. S. (1982). *The empathic communicator.* Waveland Press.

Hull, J. G., & Young, R. D. (1983). The self-awareness-reducing effects of alcohol: Evidence and implications. In J. Suls & A. Greenwald (Eds.), *Psychological perspectives on the self* (vol. 2, pp. 159–190). Lawrence Erlbaum Associates.

Inder, A. (2017). An engine of intentionality: How consciously informed agency defies the odds. *Education Today AU. 17*(2). https://www.educationtoday.com.au/news-detail/An-Engine-of-Intentionality-4888

James, W. (1890). *Principles of psychology* (2 vols.). Henry Holt.

Jones, T. (2020, June 18). *The post pandemic professional learning community*. Education Today AU. https://www.educationtoday.com.au/news-detail/--The-Post-Pandemic-Professional-Learning-Community--4956

Jourard, S. M. (1968). *Disclosing man to himself*. Van Nostrand.

Jourard, S. M. (1971). *Self-disclosure: An experimental analysis of the transparent self*. Wiley-Interscience.

Juhnke, G. A., Granello, D. H., & Granello, P. F. (2020). *School bullying and violence: Interventions for school mental health specialists*. Oxford University Press.

Kahneman, D. (2011). *Thinking, Fast and Slow*. Macmillan.

Kamenetz, A. (2015). *The test: Why our schools are obsessed with standardized testing—But you don't have to be*. PublicAffairs.

Kegan, R. (1982.) *The evolving self: Problem and process in human development*. Harvard University Press.

Kelly, G. A. (1955). *The psychology of personal constructs* (Vols. 1 & 2). W. W. Norton.

Key concepts: Toxic stress. (n.d.). Center on the Developing Child, Harvard University. Retrieved April 1, 2020 from https://developingchild.harvard.edu/science/key-concepts/toxic-stress/

Klein, G. (2016, May 1). Mindsets. *Psychology Today*. https://www.psychologytoday.com/us/blog/seeing-what-others-dont/201605/mindsets

Learning journey 3. (2018, September 18). Clarkson Community High School, Perth, AU. https://www.clarksonchs.wa.edu.au/index.php/docman-home/published-articles/160-clarkson-chs-learning-journey-3

Lecky, P. (1945). *Self-consistency: A theory of personality*. Island Press.

Levitt, S. D., & Dubner, S. J. (2014). *Think like a freak: The authors of freakonomics offer to retrain your brain*. William Morrow.

Liebman, J. L. (1946). *Peace of mind*. Simon & Schuster.

Ligonde, J. (2016). Creating a culture of peace in middle school from the inside out. *Invitational Education Forum, 37*(1), 6–12.

Lockwood, R., Allen, T., & Chicone, R. (July 2014). *Invitational Online Teaching Assessment (IOTA)*. http://invitationaledonline.com Manning, J. (1959). *Discipline in the good old days*. Phi Delta Kappa, *42*(3), 87–92.

Mansfield, D. (1999, February 24). *Boy releases principal as hostage*. Associated Press. https://apnews.com/a4453ee779ea4e73fcf231569639cfe3

Marquez, G. G. (1988). *Love in the time of cholera*. Alfred Knopf Borzoi.

Marsh, H. W. (1993). The multidimensional structure of academic self-concept: Invariance over gender and age. *American Educational Research Journal, 30*, 841–860.

Masters, E. L. (1922). *Spoon River anthology*. Macmillan.

Mead, G. H. (1934). *Mind, self and society*. University of Chicago Press.

Meichenbaum, D. (1977). *Cognitive behavior modification: An integrative approach*. Plenum Press.

Moore, S. (2017). *One without the other: Stories of unity through diversity and inclusion*. Portage & Main.

Mueller, C. M., & Dweck, C. S. (1998). Intelligence praise can undermine motivation and performance. *Journal of Personality and Social Psychology, 75*, 33–52.

Noddings, N. (1984). *Caring: A feminine approach to ethics and moral education*. University of California Press.

National Policy Board for Educational Administration (2015). Professional Standards for Educational Leaders 2015.

Noddings, N. (1993). *Educating for intelligent belief or unbelief*. Teachers College Press.

Noddings, N. (2005). *The challenge to care in schools: An alternative approach to education* (2nd ed.). Teachers College Press.

Novak, J. M., Rocca, W., & DiBiase, A. (2006). *Creating inviting schools*. Caddo Gap Press.

Novak, J. M., Armstrong, D.E., & Browne, B. (2014). *Leading for educational lives: Inviting and sustaining imaginative acts of hope in a connected world*. Sense.

Nozick, R. (1989). *The examined life: Philosophical meditations*. Simon & Schuster.

Nussbaum, M. (2010). *Not for profit: Why democracy needs the humanities*. Princeton University Press.

Ouchi, W. G. (1981). *Theory Z: How American business can meet the Japanese challenge*. Addison-Wesley.

Pajares, F. M. (1992). Teacher's beliefs and educational research: Cleaning up a messy construct. *Review of Educational Research, 62*, 329.

Patterson, C. H. (1973). *Humanistic education*. Prentice-Hall.

Payne, R. K. (2018). *A framework for understanding poverty: A cognitive approach*. aha! Process.

Pinker, S. (2011). *Toward the better angels of our nature: Why violence is declining*. Penguin.

Pinker, S. (2018): *Enlightenment now: The case for reason, science, humanism, and progress*. Penguin Random House.

Powers, W. T. (1973.) *Behavior: The control of perception*. Aldine.

Prevention Institute. (n.d.). *Preventing and reducing school violence* (Fact Sheet #3). https://www.preventioninstitute.org/sites/default/files/publications/Strategies%20resources%20and%20contacts%20for%20developing%20comprehensive%20school%20violence%20prevention%20programs.pdf

Purkey, W. W. (2000). *What students say to themselves: Internal dialogue and school success*. Corwin Press.

Purkey, W. W. (2006). *Teaching class clowns (And what they can teach us)*. Corwin Press.

Purkey, W. W. (2015, September). *An introduction to invitational theory*. Retrieved from: https://www.invitationaleducation.org/wp-content/uploads/2019/04/art_intro_to_invitational_theory-1.pdf

Purkey, W. W. (2015, December). *An introduction to the metaphor of blue and orange cards*. Retrieved July 11, 2020 at https://www.invitationaleducation.org/wp-content/uploads/2019/04/art_intro_metaphor_blue_orange_card-1.pdf.

Purkey, W. W. (2017). *Creating a positive school climate: 100 nuts & bolts of Invitational Education*. International Alliance for Invitational Education.

Purkey, W. W., Cage, B., & Graves, W. H. (1973). The Florida Key: A scale to infer learner self-concept. *Journal of Educational and Psychological Measurement*, 33(4), 979–984.

Purkey, W. W., & Novak, J. M. (1993). The Invitational HELIX: A systemic guide for individual and organizational development. *Journal of Invitational Theory and Practice*, 2(2), 59–67.

Purkey, W. W., & Novak, J. M. (2008, 2016). *Fundamentals of invitational education*. International Alliance for Invitational Education.

Purkey, W. W., Schmidt, J., & Novak, J. M. (2010). *From conflict to conciliation: How to defuse difficult situations*. Corwin Press.

Purkey, W. W., & Siegel, B. L. (2013). *Becoming an invitational leader*. Humanix Books.

Purkey, W. W., & Stanley, P. H. (1990, May/June). A blue and orange card metaphor for counselors. *Journal of Counseling and Development*, 68, 587.

Purkey, W. W., & Strahan, D. B. (2002). *Inviting positive classroom discipline*. National Middle School Association.

Riley, J. W. (1916). *James Whitcomb Riley's complete works: Vol. 5*. Bobbs-Merrill.

Ripley, D. K. (1986). Invitational teaching behavior in the associate degree clinical setting. *Journal of Nursing Education*, 25, 240–246.

Roderick, M. (1994). Grade retention and school dropout: Investigating the association. *American Educational Research Journal*, 31(4), 729–759.

Rogers, C. R. (1947). Some observations on the organization of personality. *American Psychologist*, 2, 358–368.

Rogers, C. R. (1951). *Client-centered therapy*. Houghton Mifflin.

Rogers, C. R. (1967). *Coming into existence*. World.

Rogers, C. R. (1969.) *Freedom to learn*. Charles E. Merrill.

Rogers, C. R. (1974). In retrospect—Forty-six years. *American Psychologist*, 29(2), 115.

Rogers, C. R. (1980). *A way of being*. Houghton Mifflin.

Rosenberg, M. B. (2015). *Nonviolent communication: A language of life*. Puddle Dancer Press.

Rosling, H. (2018): *Factfulness: Ten reasons why we are wrong about the world—and why things are better than we think*. Flatiron Books.

Samples, E. (May 18, 2018). Teacher pay, guns in schools loom large this election year (Florida Voices). Retrieved on April 23, 2020 from https://www.tcpalm.com/story/news/local/florida-voices/2018/05/10/teacher-election-issues-florida-voices/574747002/

Schunk, D. H. (1989). Social cognitive theory and self-regulating learning. In B. J. Zimmerman & D. H. Schunk (Eds.), *Self-regulated learning and academic achievement: Theory, research and practice* (pp. 83–110). Springer-Verlag.

Schunk, D. H. (1990). Goal setting and self-efficacy during self-regulated learning. *Educational Psychologist, 25*, 70–86.

Segal, Z. V., Williams, J. M., & Teasdale, J. D. (2013). *Mindfulness-based cognitive therapy for depression* (2nd ed.). Guilford Press.

Seligman, M. E. (1975). *Helplessness: On depression, development, and death.* W. H. Freeman.

Seligman, M. E. (2006). *Learned optimism: How to change your mind and your life.* Vintage.

Seligman, M. E. (2011). *Flourish.* Simon & Schuster.

Sergiovanni, T. J. (1994). *Building community in schools.* Jossey-Bass.

Shavelson, R. J., & Marsh, H. W. (1986). On the structure of self-concept. In R. Schwartzer (Ed.), *Anxiety and cognition* (pp. 305–330). Erlbaum Associates.

Shoffner, M. F., & Vacc, N. A. (1999). Psychometric analysis of the Inviting School Safety Survey. *Measurement and Evaluation in Counseling and Development, 32*(2), 66–74.

Siegel, D. J. (1999). *The developing mind: Toward a neurobiology of interpersonal experience.* Guilford Press.

Siegel, D. J. (2007). *The mindful brain: Reflection and attunement in the cultivation of well-being* (Norton Series on Interpersonal Neurobiology). Norton and Company.

Siegel, D. J. (2010). *Mindsight.* Bantam.

Siegel, D. J. (2014.) *Brainstorm: The power and purpose of the teenage brain.* Penguin Publishing

Siegel, D. J. (2018). *Aware: The science and practice of presence.* Penguin Random House.

Siegel, D. J., & Bryson, T. P. (2020). *The power of showing up.* Ballantine.

Smith, K. (2016). *Manual for the Inviting School Survey: A survey for measuring the invitational qualities (IQ) of the total school climate* (4th ed.). International Alliance for Invitational Education.

Snygg, D., & Combs, A. W. (1949). *Individual behavior: A new frame of reference for psychology.* Harper & Row.

Stanley, P. H. (1991). *Asymmetry in internal dialogue, core assumptions, and counselor trainee effectiveness* (Unpublished doctoral dissertation). The University of North Carolina at Greensboro.

Taylor, S. E. (1989). *Positive illusions: Creative self-deceptions and the healthy mind.* Basic Books.

Tesser, A., & Campbell, J. (1983). Self-definition and self-evaluation maintenance. In J. Suls & A. Greenwald (Eds.), *Psychological perspectives on the self* (Vol. 2, pp. 1–31). Lawrence Erlbaum Associates.

Turner, H., Finkelhor, D., Ormrod, R., & Hamby, S. (2009) Violence, abuse, and crime exposure in a national sample of children and youth. *Pediatrics, 124*(5), 1411–1423.

Wenger, E. (2000). *Communities of practice: Learning, meaning, and identity*. Cambridge University Press.

White, T. H. (1958). *The once and future king*. Putnam.

Wood, C., & Freeman-Loftis, B. (2015). *Responsive school discipline: Essentials for elementary school leaders*. Center for Responsive Teaching.

Ybrandt, H. (2008, February 1). The relation between self-concept and social functioning in adolescence. *Journal of Adolescence, 31*(1), 1–16. https://doi .org/10.1016/j.adolescence.2007.03.004

Zimmerman, B. J., Bandura, A., & Martinez-Pons, M. (1992). Self-motivation for academic attainment: The role of self-efficacy beliefs and personal goal setting. *American Educational Research Journal, 29*, 663–676.

Zimmerman, I. L., & Allebrand, G. N. (1965). Personality characteristics and attitudes toward achievement of good and poor readers. *The Journal of Educational Research, 59*, 28–30.

Index

The letter *f* after a page number indicates a figure.

About the Authors

Dr. William Watson Purkey is professor emeritus of counselor education at the University of North Carolina at Greensboro. He is internationally recognized for his research and writing on self-concept theory and human motivation. His most recent research is on defusing difficult challenges in education. Author of 10 books on school climate, his major works include *Self Concept and School Achievement* (Prentice-Hall) and *Inviting School Success* (Wadsworth).

Dr. John Michael Novak is professor emeritus of education at Brock University, St. Catharines, Ontario, Canada. An invited speaker on six continents, he is also a past president of the Society of Professors of Education and a former member of the Executive Board of the John Dewey Society. He has written a dozen books and monographs, including *Leading for Educational Lives* (Sense Publishers) and *Inviting Educational Leadership* (Pearson).

Joan R. Fretz is a school climate consultant, providing trainings in the New York metropolitan area and throughout the United States, Canada, and Hong Kong. A veteran school administrator and teacher, Joan helps schools create positive climates by using an invitational framework, and by integrating strategies such as mindful communication, social and emotional learning, and collaborative solutions to challenging behaviors. She served as the executive director of the International Alliance for Invitational Education, is a Lions Quest Social and Emotional Learning Program trainer, and is cofounder of the Long Island SEL Forum. Access Joan's resources at https://joanfretz.com.